THE
OAK
ISLAND
MYSTERY

THE
OAK ISLAND MYSTERY

*The Secret of the
World's Greatest Treasure Hunt*

LIONEL & PATRICIA FANTHORPE

HOUNSLOW

The Oak Island Mystery : The Secret of the World's Greatest Treasure Hunt

Copyright © 1995 by Lionel & Patricia Fanthorpe

All rights reserved. No part of this publication may be reproduced, stored in a retrieval system, or transmitted in any form or by any means, electronic, mechanical, photo-copying, recording, or otherwise (except brief passages for purposes of review) without the prior permission of Hounslow Press. Permission to photocopy should be requested from the Canadian Reprography Collective.

HOUNSLOW PRESS
A member of the Dundurn Group

Publishers: Kirk Howard & Anthony Hawke
Printer: Metrolitho Inc., Quebec
Front cover photograph: Sky-Shots Inc., Chester, Nova Scotia

Canadian Cataloguing in Publication Data
Fanthorpe, R. Lionel
    The Oak Island mystery : the secret of the world's greatest treasure hunt

Includes bibliographical references.

ISBN 0-88882-170-0

1. Oak Island (N.S.). 2. Treasure-trove - Nova Scotia - Oak Island.
3. Oak Island Treasure Site (N.S.).
I. Fanthorpe, Patricia. II. Title

FC2345.023F36 1994   971.6' 23   C94-931401-3
F1039.035F36 1994

Care has been taken to trace the ownership of copyright material used in this book. The author and publisher welcome any information enabling them to rectify any references or credit in subsequent editions.

Hounslow Press   Hounslow Press   Hounslow Press
8 Market Street   73 Lime Walk   250 Sonwil Drive
Suite 200   Headington, Oxford   Buffalo, NY
Toronto, Ontario, Canada England   U.S.A. 14225
M5E 1M6   OX3 7AD

Printed and bound in Canada

Second printing: February 1998

This book is dedicated to our special friends

Dr. Bob and Zoh Hieronimus,

their daughter Anna, and

Laura Cortner,

in appreciation of their kindness and admiration
for their professional work.

CONTENTS

FOREWORD

The coming of television has no doubt made a difference but at one time card parties were for many years a feature of family life. Not many households were without packs of cards, fifty-two in each pack divided equally between Clubs, Diamonds, Hearts and Spades. The choice of such symbols was perhaps purely arbitrary on the part of the original designers, but in themselves they represent some of the basic impulses by which human nature has been consistently driven. Whether intended or not they represent very real motives for living.

Some love power. They rise to the top. They struggle for authority. Woe betide any lesser mortals who dare to get in their way. The Club is their natural symbol. Others accumulate money as their life's ambition. Diamonds may be a girl's best friend but getting rich attracts ambitious people of both sexes and all ages. For others the only conceivable inspiration for life is love, the kind which is gentle, compassionate and self-sacrificing. St Francis of Assisi became one of them and Mother Teresa of Calcutta is another. There are others like them, always have been and always will be. Their symbol is the heart. For another grouping work is the mainspring of their lives. They know nothing else; they value nothing else. It could be said of one, 'He was born a man; he died a grocer.' All else is subordinated to work: good name, health, family, all, in their turn, sacrificed to it. For this group the natural symbol is the Spade.

By such motives, in lesser or greater degrees, our people are driven. But these are not the only driving forces that take control of us. There are others just as all-consuming and one such is curiosity. A cat is said to have nine lives but curiosity is the thing most likely to kill it. Dangerous for the cats of this world it may be but without its driving force many of our advances in life and much of our knowledge would have been far slower in arriving.

It was our curiosity, the desire to know, that led Christopher Columbus over unknown seas to the New World, and curiosity that compelled him to continue in spite of having to use ships inadequate for such long voyages and rough seas, and discontented frightened sailors to man them. He was driven ever onwards to discover what lay beyond the horizon.

It was the desire to know that led Lord Carnarvon and Howard Carter through years of frustration and failure until one day they discovered in the Valley of the Kings the tomb of Tutankhamen, and, within it, the most complete collection of funeral trappings and properties in the whole history of Egyptology.

It was the desire to know at all costs that led to the search for electric power, immunisation against disease and success, finally, in landing men on the surface of the moon. Curiosity has been one of the greatest impulses of life, driving people into uncharted territory, over unknown seas, and all with no thought of surrender whatever the odds.

Curiosity on its own then is one of the great driving forces of life. When allied to certain other motives, some good some bad, it becomes even more formidable. Greed and perseverance can often be found associated with it, and no more so than in the long struggle to penetrate the mystery of Oak Island and the so-called Money Pit.

In the early years the searching of Oak Island appears to have been dominated mostly by curiosity, the simple and uncomplicated desire to know what was to be found there. The young men who first found the Pit, all of them under twenty years of age, were initially simply intrigued by what they saw. They found, in a forest clearing, a sunken indentation wide enough to resemble the head of a large well, and above it the remains of a ship's tackle block, suspended from the branch of a large oak tree cut to support it. As they began to dig and found first a slab of stone and later several wooden platforms the desire to know what lay beneath them grew ever greater. At this stage there seems no desire to grow rich from what they hoped to find.

The fortune hunters followed in later years, earning the area the name of the Money Pit, though as far as is known, no money as yet has ever been found in it. For over two hundred years vastly more money has been poured into it than anything of value ever secured from it.

To curiosity and greed a third great impulse has clearly been at work on Oak Island. It is the human gift of perseverance. Without that gift some of our greatest achievements and discoveries would never have happened as soon as they did. Perseverance enabled Columbus to reach the New World. It led Livingstone through parts of Africa never yet explored. It brought the 1953 party to the summit of Everest where others before them had lost their lives in the struggle. Perseverance tends to pay off in the end but not on Oak Island, not with the Money Pit. For two hundred years now groups have been trying to penetrate its secrets, using ever more advanced techniques in mining engineering with ever greatly increased financial backing and with the experience of so many failed attempts to work on and yet nothing tangible has been found for all their efforts. Families down several generations have been drawn to it and ruined by it. There has been a battle of wits between the unknown master engineers who it seems buried something and then devised a scheme which would thwart all attempts to reach it. Curiosity, greed and perseverance, have all hammered against it, from the simple pick and shovel, to the sophisticated pump, even to dynamite. But he who designed the defences has foiled them all. So intense has been the struggle, so insistent the effort, even the exact area of the Money Pit is now difficult to identify.

The Reverend Lionel Fanthorpe and his wife, Patricia, the authors of this study, have come to it soon after their struggles to unravel the mystery of the sudden unexplained wealth of the once impoverished Priest of Rennes-le-Château, Bérenger Saunière. Their researches in Rennes were deep, widespread and continued over many years. Nothing was left untested and every theory examined with care and scholarship. In the end, however, those of us who enjoyed the book[1] and marvelled at the scholarship were bound to say that the last word still lay with the old Priest. He found riches somewhere and in abundance, beyond even our wildest dreams, but he took the secret of this wealth with him into the grave.

The true scholar spares little thought for treasure. He doesn't expect to be rich but he is desperate to find the truth. The authors of this book have laid bare the facts. Something of value was brought to Oak Island and was protected by someone at some time. Whoever he was he used the waters of the sea as his protective shield. What was it he buried? Is it still there to be found? If so how can his ingenious mechanism be diverted? Have the waters, so to speak, now been so muddied, the ground around so devastated, as to render discovery impossible?

You will enjoy reading this book as I have. What or whom will you admire most? The ghostly engineer whose skill has so far outwitted everyone? The fortune hunters whose persistence engulfed years of their lives and drew most of their money down into the shaft only to surrender all of it to the waters? Or shall we rather admire those who for no financial gain whatever have been proud to devote their time, their energy, their cleverness to a study of the chase and the frustrations of all those who took part in it? The builders of the Pit, the treasure seekers, the research historians are all heroes in this work. There is a record here of ingenuity at its most baffling. Perhaps in the Preface, as with the Island, the last word should be allowed to the engineer-inventor of long ago. He may be saying to himself somewhere in another life, "They have had the Pit all these years. They had all those resources to use. They had so many failures to learn from," and then with a smile,

---

1 R.L. and P.A. Fanthorpe, *Secrets of Rennes-le-Château* (York Beach, Maine: Samuel Weiser Inc., 1992).

if smiles still feature in life eternal, he may add, "but none of them has ever got to the treasure and they never will."

Canon Stanley H. Mogford[2], M.A.,
Cardiff, Wales, U.K. 1994

---

2 One of Lionel Fanthorpe's Theology Tutors during Ordination Training, Canon Mogford is rightly renowned and widely respected throughout the Church in Wales for his profound wisdom, wide experience and extensive scholarship. The authors are deeply grateful to him for reading the manuscript and enriching their book with this foreword.

Acknowledgements

We are very grateful indeed to Dan Blankenship and family for all their hospitality, expert help and advice, and to their friend and colleague Dan Henskee, during our site research on Oak Island.

Many thanks to Jim Sedgewick of Skyshots Aerial Photography, 4073 #3 Highway, P.O. Box 2000, Chester, Nova Scotia, BOJ 1JO, for his friendly and wholehearted co-operation and brilliant photographic professionalism.

We owe a great deal to George Young's enthusiastic support, his vast experience in so many relevant fields and his exciting new ideas, and to his wife, Janette, for her unfailing hospitality during our visits to their lovely home in Nova Scotia.

Much gratitude to our other hosts in Nova Scotia, Jeanne and Ned Nash, who did so much to help us, and whose very comfortable and welcoming Stoney Brook Guest House, in Chester, was always a pleasure to visit.

Many thanks to our friend, Canon Stanley Mogford, M.A., for writing the Foreword. Canon Mogford is very well-known and greatly respected throughout the Church in Wales for his wit, wisdom, wealth of academic experience and scholarly prowess. We're also deeply grateful to our publishers, Kirk Howard and Tony Hawke, for their interest in our ideas, their valuable suggestions, their confidence, their encouragement, and their generous hospitality while we were in Toronto.

Last, but by no means least, we are greatly indebted to our friend Paul V. S. Townsend, M.Sc., unsurpassable computer 'wizard,' cryptographer, problem-solver, meticulous typesetter, eagle-eyed proof-reader, and ingenious compiler of footnotes and other improvements to our text.

Lionel and Patricia Fanthorpe
Cardiff, Wales, U.K. 1994

Introduction

The mystery of the Oak Island Money Pit is equalled only by the riddle of whatever it was that Father Bérenger Saunière and Marie Dénarnaud found at Rennes-le-Château a century ago, and by Monsieur Fradin's amazing discoveries at Glozel near Vichy in 1924.

In some ways all three stories are remarkably similar: in one vital respect they are very different. Whatever else may be in doubt about the Rennes mystery, Saunière had access to vast wealth — and for over thirty years he was a singularly conspicuous consumer. With the possible exception of John Pitblado (Pitbladdo in some accounts) no one has yet found — let alone spent — any of the Oak Island treasure; and the mysterious Glozel inscriptions have yet to be deciphered.

The heart of the Nova Scotian enigma is a very deep shaft sunk into Oak Island which lies just off the coast of Chester, in Mahone Bay, in Lunenburg County. Roughly thirty-three metres below the surface are what appear to be two cunningly designed flood tunnels which link the shaft to the Atlantic Ocean. Augmented by a subterranean river, these flood tunnels have so far defeated every attempt to recover whatever may lie buried at the foot of the mysterious old shaft, and those attempts have now been going on for almost two hundred years.

The modern part of the story begins in 1795. One summer afternoon Daniel McGinnis, who was then a teenaged farm boy, rowed out to explore uninhabited Oak Island. He came across a small clearing in which was a saucer shaped depression about four metres across. Beside it stood an oak with one sturdy branch lopped off to correspond with the centre of the hollow. An old ship's block and tackle hung from this lopped branch. Daniel fetched two friends in his own age group: John Smith and Anthony Vaughan. The lads began to dig. They soon realised that they were re-excavating a circular shaft. The tough clay walls clearly bore the pick marks of whoever had dug the shaft original-ly. Within a metre of the surface the boys discovered a layer of stone slabs, the rock from which the slabs were cut was not of a type found on the island. It had apparently come from Gold River about three kilometres up the mainland coast.

As if the Gold River slabs and pick marks in the clay were not evidence enough of the shaft's importance, three metres down the boys struck a platform of transverse oak logs embedded firmly in the clay walls of the shaft. The outer surfaces were decaying: the oak platform had evi-dently been there a long time. The boys prised it out and discovered that the soil below it had settled to leave a verti-cal gap of about half a metre. Encouraged by the thought that such elaborate and laborious work probably concealed a very considerable treasure, they dug on with renewed enthusiasm. Between the six-and-seven metre levels they encountered another transverse oak platform; between nine and ten metres down they found another platform.

Realising that an excavation on this scale was more than they could handle, the lads decided to call on adult relatives and friends to help.

That small beginning was almost two centuries ago. During the intervening years many ingenious and coura-geous mining engineers — often equipped with the latest technology and pumping equipment — have attempted to solve the mystery. So far — all have failed. Like Rennes-le-Château and Glozel, Oak Island refuses to give up its secret.

Our site investigations on Oak Island itself, and on neighbouring Frog Island — where there appears to be a similar shaft which may well be linked to Oak Island — together with our local interviews and other research, have led us to consider seven major possibilities:

a) that the Money Pit was constructed to hold several substantial British Army pay chests (dating from the American War of Independence) to keep them safe from the Americans and their French allies;

b) that it was the work of Sir Francis Drake's men in the sixteenth century and was built to hold captured Spanish gold;

c) that it was dug by William Kidd, or some other privateer or pirate, during the seventeenth century;

d)   that it was constructed as the tomb of an Arif, or Holy Man, who had led a party of religious refugees over the Atlantic to Nova Scotia — this is George Young's fascinating hypothesis;

e) that it was built four centuries ago to house precious original manuscripts, possibly even the controversial works of Francis Bacon;

f) that it was constructed by Norsemen, or early Welsh sea rovers, perhaps as a royal burial place;

g) that it was constructed to conceal part of the mysterious Rennes-le-Château 'Arcadian Treasure' possibly brought from Europe by Verrazano in the 1530s, and that the strange coded stone of Oak Island is also linked with the weird alphabet at Glozel and the Rennes cyphers.

This raises the question of what the core of that Arcadian Treasure really was. Could it have been a mysterious artifact from ancient Egypt which travelled through one treasure house after another until the Templars got possession of it? Did they, rather than Verrazano, carry it across the Atlantic with the help of Prince Henry Sinclair?

The quest begins with two basic facts and two basic questions. There is a deep shaft on Oak Island which was either man-made, or man-adapted long ago. There are at least two flood tunnels connecting the lower parts of this shaft to the Atlantic. These, too, were either man-made or man-adapted.

The first question is: who created, or modified, the shaft and its flood tunnels? The second question is: why?

As with the mysteries of Rennes-le-Château and Glozel, there are no quick, simple or certain answers — only a range of greater or lesser possibilities. It is the authors' intention to lay those possibilities and speculations before our readers, together with such relevant evidence as exists, and such arguments and deductions as may reasonably be based on that evidence. It is also the authors' intention to indicate which hypothesis they themselves think is the most probable and to give reasons for their choice.

Lionel and Patricia Fanthorpe
Cardiff, Wales, U.K. 1994

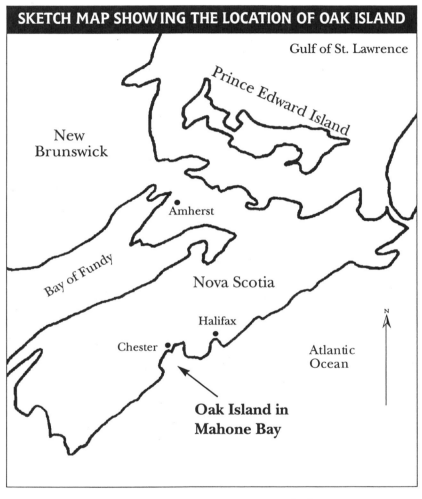

SKETCH MAP SHOWING THE LOCATION OF OAK ISLAND

Gulf of St. Lawrence

Prince Edward Island

New
Brunswick

Amherst

Bay of Fundy

Nova Scotia

Halifax

N

Chester

Atlantic
Ocean

**Oak Island in
Mahone Bay**

Scale

100 Miles

1

OAK ISLAND AND ITS BACKGROUND

If you spent just one day on each island in Mahone Bay it would take a year to explore them all. Oak Island is not short of neighbours.

A mile long and slightly less than half that width, it narrows in the centre where the swamp lies. Viewed from the east, the island is reminiscent of the curiously shaped puff of smoke which emerges from Aladdin's Lamp in the cartoons and then turns into a genie. The Oak Island genie (if he is still there!) has remained stubbornly concealed at the bottom of his flooded Money Pit.

The current name, Oak Island, seems to be based on the presence of the red oaks with their characteristic umbrella-shaped domes. At one time they were far more numerous than they are today. A chart drawn by a British cartographer named Des Barres in the last quarter of the eighteenth century calls the island Glouster Isle and names today's Mahone Bay as Mecklenburgh Bay. In spite of Des Barres' nomenclature, however, some legal documents which are older than his chart refer to the island as Oak Island.

The highest points of Oak Island barely rise ten metres above the surface of the Atlantic. These high points are drumlins, miniature hills of very hard clay inherited from the Ice Age. Below them Oak Island stands on limestone. Geologically, there are several significant features which are worth careful consideration: the hard clay, for example, is firm enough to be excavated to a considerable depth without any lateral supports being used; and it is also practically impervious to water seepage. Our friend George Young, a professional surveyor in the district for many years, knows a great deal about the characteristics of the local limestone. In his long and extensive experience he has encountered many curious natural holes, caverns, shafts and connecting passageways in the geological formations surrounding Oak Island. The mysterious Money Pit, with its ancillary system of tunnels and vaults, may actually be an adaptation rather than an entirely artificial structure.

The island's longer dimension runs from west to east, the western end having been linked to the mainland by a causeway since 1965. The Money Pit is close to the eastern, or Atlantic, side. That part of the island, on the seaward side of the central swamp, is bleak, scarred by craters and the frequently disturbed earth of many old excavations. The rest of it supports the usual island grass, trees and shrubs. There are interesting ruins here and there, together with a small museum where core samples from exploratory drillings and unearthed artifacts are on display.

Halifax, seventy kilometres north of Oak Island, was established as early as 1749. Lunenburg, fifteen kilometres south-west of the island, was settled in 1753.

In October 1759, Charles Lawrence, who was then the Governor-General of Nova Scotia, included Oak Island in the Shoreham Grant. This grant established the town of Shoreham (which is now Chester) seven kilometres northeast of Oak Island. There is an interesting possibility that this same Lawrence family may have had connections with Rennes-le-Château via the curious tomb at Arques, which was a facsimile of the one in Poussin's famous painting "Bergeres d'Arcadie" until it was deliberately demolished by the new owner in the late 1980s. This facsimile tomb was constructed nearly a century ago on the orders of an American emigrant named Lawrence who settled near

Rennes-le-Château. Records indicate that his wife and mother were buried in it, and when we ourselves photographed the interior in the 1970s there were certainly two coffins at the bottom.

Oak Island then became the possession of four families: the Monros, the Lynches, the Seacombes and the Youngs (possibly, George's ancestors), although it was not inhabited when Daniel McGinnis landed there thirty-six years later in 1795. It is no longer possible to state with any degree of certainty how those four farming families used the island, but, in all probability, they would have pastured some of their livestock there. (Island pasturage had the advantage of not needing to be fenced, and, in the normal course of events, the small islands in Mahone Bay would have been free of predators.) In the eighteenth century, when the oaks were still plentiful, the island might also have been a useful source of timber.

The earliest known survey would seem to have been the work of Charles Morris, who was then working as an official surveyor in the area. His charts divided the island into thirty-two parcels of land of about four acres each: the first twenty ranged along the northern edge; the last twelve were along the southern shore.

Early records show that Timothy Lynch purchased land parcel number nineteen from Edward Smith in 1768. (Smith's Cove may have got its name from this same Edward Smith.) Lynch's Plot Nineteen was well towards the eastern tip of Oak Island, adjacent to Plot Eighteen which held the mysterious "Money Pit." The John Smith (apparently no relation to Edward) who was one of the three original discoverers of the Money Pit in 1795, paid £7.10.0 for Plot Eighteen on June 26 of that year.

Presumably, he did this immediately after the three lads had begun their pioneering dig. The former owner is listed as a Casper Wollenhaupt of Lunenburg. Despite Oak Island's sinister local reputation then as a haunt of murderous pirates (and worse), young John Smith took his wife and family to live there and thrived for another sixty years.

Curious rumours of dark supernatural forces on Oak Island were reinforced by a legend that during the mid-eighteenth century the citizens of Chester had seen strange lights burning persistently on Oak Island by night. It was also darkly hinted that two Chester fishermen who had rowed across to investigate had never been seen again.

Oak Island does seem to possess an atmosphere of subtle mystery and intrigue. Looking out across Smith's Cove, where the fan-shaped entrance to one of the sinister flood tunnels still lies somewhere beneath the artificial beach, the researcher ponders over who might have constructed

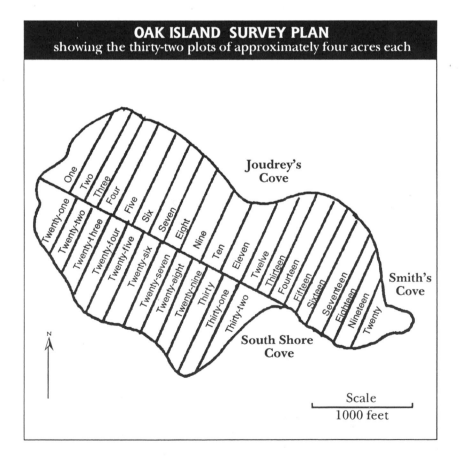

OAK ISLAND SURVEY PLAN
showing the thirty-two plots of approximately four acres each

this whole weird system, and why. Driving by moonlight across the 200-metre causeway separating Oak Island from Crandall's Point on the mainland is also an evocative experience.

But 'atmospheres' are notoriously deceptive and subjective. Whether the feeling of enigmatic mystery in the air of Oak Island has any objective reality, or whether the visitors' knowledge of the island's strange history generates the atmosphere is an argument which is not easy to resolve.

What other background information might contribute usefully and relevantly to an analysis of the mystery of the Oak Island Money Pit? How much attention needs to be paid to the climate, the geography and geology of Nova Scotia itself to gain a fair background for studying the Money Pit?

Just as Rome and Constantinople were traditionally built on seven hills, so Nova Scotia is built on five; five upland areas and five lowlands. The raised areas are based on hard, crystalline rocks and consist of: the Southern Upland which doesn't rise above 600 feet; the narrow, flat-topped North Mountain, which reaches about the same height and runs alongside the Bay of Fundy; the Cobequid Mountains, which are nearly 300 feet higher and cross Cumberland County; the Pictou and Antigonish Highlands; and, fifth, the Cape Breton Highlands which reach approximately 1200 feet. The five lowland areas have soft, sedimentary rocks beneath them.

The mineral wealth of Nova Scotia includes lead, zinc, silver and copper in the Bathurst area of New Brunswick, and coal in the northern part of Cape Breton Island.

Nova Scotia must also be considered as a mass of lakes, streams and unusually short rivers — while the subterranean water courses may be larger and more extensive than is generally realised. The curiously named Lake Bras d'Or (Golden Arm Lake) on Cape Breton Island, for example, is saline.

The Nova Scotian climate is a strange mixture in that it is both continental and oceanic. The south-west coast in particular tends to be mild and wet, and its average temperature is roughly five degrees warmer than the average interior temperature (approximately 45°F and 40°F respectively). The upland temperatures can range from 95°F in summer down to 35° of frost in winter — a remarkably wide range of 125 F°. There's an annual rainfall of between 40 and 55 inches, and fog can hide the southern coasts for as many as ninety days a year. There are upwards of 50,000 acres of tidal marshland in Nova Scotia, and it's particularly interesting to note that it was the Acadians who began creating dikes around the turn of the seventeenth century.

With its fogs and sinister tidal marshes, the Nova Scotian coast was a haven for pirates, and Mahone Bay itself was notorious for its pirates, privateers and buccaneers right up until the early years of the eighteenth century. The scores of scattered islands there provided ideal screening and camouflage from both sea and land. Expert anthropological opinion suggests that the earliest inhabitants were the Amerindian tribes who were contemporaries of the old Chaldean civilisations, and pre-dated Stonehenge, the pyramids and the Sphinx. But these palaeolithic tribes — or even their mesolithic or neolithic descendants — were not characterised by their mining or constructional activities. Radio carbon dating of what are thought to be some of the 'original' Money Pit timbers produces a date not earlier than 1500 — although even the best radio carbon techniques can leave a few years' margin of doubt. There may very well be much older remains on the site.

About 700 years after the dawn of the Christian Era the Micmac Indians seem to have migrated northwards into Nova Scotia from what is now the U.S.A. While William the Conqueror was getting a firm grip on England several thousand Micmacs were spreading themselves around the coastal area adjacent to Oak Island and its hinterland.

But the Micmacs were a travelling people — like the Bedouins of Arabia and North Africa. They carried their homes and their few goods with them and they tended to travel light. There is no known motive — religious or cultural — which might have induced them to construct the elaborate system below Oak Island.

Although the theory is still controversial with some of the more cautious and conservative historians, it now seems virtually certain that Vikings — and some formidable wild Welsh sea warriors — reached North America and Canada centuries before Columbus. Was the mysterious 'Wineland' or 'Vinland' which Lief Ericsson reputedly reached one thousand years ago really Nova Scotia? Thorfinn Karlsefni took three shiploads of adventurous pioneers to an equally mysterious 'Markland' a few years after Lief Ericsson's epic voyage. Was 'Markland' also Nova Scotia?

Men who could build ships sturdy enough to be rowed across the Atlantic would have been more than capable of excavating or adapting the subterranean system on Oak Island — but what might their motives have been? Norsemen, of course, were not averse to burying dead kings and chieftains complete with their ships and their treasures. Visigoths habitually diverted rivers to bury their great leaders, then let the waters flood back to protect the tomb and the king's wealth.

If the radio carbon dating is five hundred years adrift, there's a remote possibility that some great Viking warlord, or Celtic sea-rover, lies below Oak Island.

John Cabot raised the English flag on Cape Breton Island before 1500, thus laying claim to what he fondly believed to be part of Eastern Asia in the name of Henry Tudor! Shortly after the turn of the century, Basques and Bretons came in search of fish.

The French Baron de Lery got to Nova Scotia before 1520, while the Italian explorer Giovanni da Verrazano made an unsuccessful attempt to found a settlement there during the third decade of the sixteenth century. Both of these visits are of very considerable significance: firstly, because any Oak Island activity undertaken by their people would harmonise with the radio carbon dating, and, secondly, because some researchers believe that Verrazano named the area "Arcadia."

To justify the importance of the word "Arcadia" we need to look briefly at another mystery. Central to the riddle of the Priest's Treasure at Rennes-le-Château in south-western France is the curious Latin phrase "Et in Arcadia ego." It recurs in old paintings and on the Shugborough Hall Shepherds' Monument, in Staffordshire in England. It also appears in the controversial coded parchments which Bérenger Saunière is said to have found inside an ancient Visigothic altar pillar in his mountain top church of St. Mary Magdalene. The classical interpretation of the cryptic Latin phrase is usually taken to be: "Even in Arcadia (the idyllic, innocent and joyful land) I, Death, am present."

Alternatively, the message, carved on the side of a table tomb in Poussin's paintings, may be taken to mean that the dead man inside the tomb is saying: "Don't grieve for me: I, too, am in Arcadia." Nicholas Poussin had a great love of Rome, and worked there for many years. Significantly, his own tomb bears a carved representation of the Shepherds of Arcadia canvas bearing the same puzzling 'Arcadia' inscription.

Art historians trace the theme back from Poussin to the Italian painter Guercino whose work on the same motif depicts a skull beside which the words "Et in Arcadia ego" appear. What if the French adventurer, Baron de Lery, or Verrazano, the Italian colonial pioneer, had a very good reason indeed for naming their respective abortive settlements "Arcadia"?

One of our Nova Scotian friends, George Young, who is himself an expert on the Oak Island mystery, came up with the brilliantly innovative idea that the characters depicted in the Poussin paintings might actually be signalling letters in the old Ogham script. It was George who drew our attention to the fact that Ogham letters are capable of being denoted by the positions of the hands and fingers —

as though Ogham were a very early progenitor of the sign language used to help those with a hearing challenge today.

What if whatever mysterious, wealth-17generating secrets were (and perhaps still are) hidden at Rennes-le-Château and/or Glozel, have some curious duplicate, counterpart or accessory hidden on the other side of the Atlantic? And what if Guercino, Poussin and the other painters who knew at least part of that secret hid ancient Ogham letters in their compositions?

What if Verrazano's apparently failed attempt to establish a colony in Nova Scotia was no failure at all but a deliberate cover, or elaborate camouflage, to enable something of immense value and importance to be concealed in the Money Pit on Oak Island?

The mind of a brilliant Renaissance Italian would have been the ideal spawning ground for the plans of the Oak Island System. Compare it with the catacombs of ancient Rome. The skill of the craftsmen who built, furnished and decorated Renaissance Italy would have been more than adequate to design and build the Money Pit. The question remains: what could have been so vitally important that they went to such lengths to transport, conceal and protect it?

During most of the seventeenth and eighteenth centuries, British and French forces fought long and hard for possession of Nova Scotia. One civil or military pay chest or another, legitimately or illegitimately, could have found its way to the base of a secret subterranean 'safe deposit' on Oak Island — if that's what the Money Pit actually was!

The massive fortress of Louisbourg at the eastern end of Cape Breton cost the French millions to build. Were some of those funds misappropriated and secretly hidden on Oak Island?

The Oak Island story may go back much further into the mists of time than is generally realised: fearless Celts, Coptic Christian refugees, grimly determined Norsemen, the noble and heroic Sinclair branch of the Knights Templar after their betrayal and downfall in 1307, Drake's

Devon lads, Kidd's bloodthirsty pirates or a detachment of meticulously disciplined British army engineers . . . Who constructed the Money Pit and why?

The historical and geological background of Oak Island and its immediate surroundings abound with exciting and intriguing possibilities.

2

SMITH, VAUGHAN AND MCGINNIS IN 1795

To understand Daniel McGinnis and his pioneering companions, it is first necessary to know something of the political and social background of Nova Scotia in the eighteenth century. The Chinese have a proverbial 'curse' which runs: "May you live in interesting times." The eighteenth century was — in that subtle Chinese sense — an interesting time to be in Nova Scotia, and particularly if you lived on, or near, its coast.

The French and English had long disputed the ownership of what was then termed "Acadie" (or, perhaps, more significantly "Acadia," "Arcadie" or "Arcadia"). Champlain had been there in 1603 and De Monts in 1604. The Treaty of Utrecht gave Acadia to the English in 1713, but in 1755 the danger of war with France led the English to deport the Acadians to New Orleans. This caused great hardship, and many personal tragedies of the kind Henry Wadsworth Longfellow described so poignantly in *Evangeline*.

There is an evocative and mysterious tone to the opening lines of the poem:

> *This is the forest primeval. The murmuring pines and the*
> *   hemlocks,*
> *Bearded with moss, and in garments green indistinct in*
> *   the twilight,*

Stand like Druids of eld, with voices sad and prophetic,
Stand like harpers hoar, with beards that rest on their
* bosoms.*
Loud from its rocky caverns, the deep voiced neighbour
* ing ocean*
Speaks, and in accents disconsolate answers the wail of
* the forest.*

Longfellow was a genius with a great interest in history and romantic legends. There is a strong suspicion that — like the even more brilliant J.R.R. Tolkien of later days — Longfellow knew rather more about the undiscovered byways of ancient history than he was prepared to say explicitly.

Another fascinating parallel can be found in the works of Victor Hugo, and in particular his *La Legende des Siècles*. In one of these epic poems, which Hugo claims are based on historical fact, he appears to be referring to the mysterious lost treasure of Rennes-le-Château, which is, in turn, connected with Oak Island. Longfellow wrote not only of the Acadians, but of Viking legends. His *Skeleton in Armour* suggests that the ancient remains found in Fall River were those of a Norseman who had built the archaeologically controversial Newport Tower on Rhode Island.

Half-way through the eighteenth century, the indigenous Micmac population of Nova Scotia was struggling against the new arrivals, and against tuberculosis. The neighbouring Americans were divided between those who wanted nationhood and independence and those who wanted to remain under the protection of the British Crown.

The Atlantic Ocean provided hazards ranging from floods and storms to pirates and privateers. Nova Scotian fishermen and farmers in those days had to be tough and resourceful in order to survive: they were — and they did.

By the second half of the century, about 6,000 of the original French settlers had been deported. They were replaced by settlers from New England, Yorkshire, Scotland and Ireland. The American element in this migration were United Empire Loyalists, and among them was Daniel

McGinnis's family. They lived alongside other United Empire Loyalists on the comparatively sheltered shores of Mahone Bay. Although life there was undeniably hard in those days, it was not without its compensations: natural resources and worthwhile opportunities abounded for those who were prepared to work.

Soil, once cleared, became good, fertile farm land. Timber was abundant and could be felled and sold, or used for building houses and ships. The sea was unpolluted and teeming with fish. Despite its hardships and dangers, Mahone Bay was a place where people could live and prosper.

On that fateful summer's day in 1795, young Daniel McGinnis was taking a few hours off work to explore some of the hundreds of islands scattered across the bay like mushrooms in a meadow. He reached Oak Island, scarcely two hundred metres off shore, and began to wander through the huge old red oaks that gave the island its name. Reaching a clearing close to the eastern end of the island, he was intrigued by a circular depression, approximately thirteen feet across. The earth here had subsided as if a wide shaft had been excavated and refilled long ago, and the soil had subsequently settled.

Above this depression stood a great oak with one large branch lopped off short so that its end was now more or less over the centre of the depression. From that shortened branch hung a very old and fragile ship's block and tackle.

Knowing the history of the area, and especially the many rumours and legends of buccaneers burying their treasure off the coast of Nova Scotia, Daniel's first thought was that this must be the top of a pirate's cache.

He went to fetch two young friends to show them what he had discovered, and it is interesting to note here that the Puritan work ethic prevailing in Nova Scotia at the time was such that Daniel felt it very unlikely that adult members of his family would have offered much encouragement. He probably suspected that he would be reprimanded for 'wasting his time on idle fancies' instead of getting on

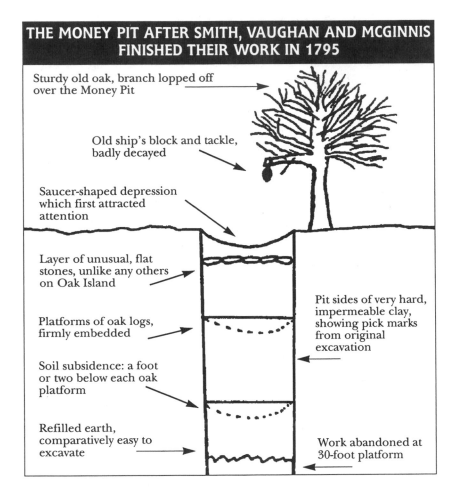

THE MONEY PIT AFTER SMITH, VAUGHAN AND MCGINNIS FINISHED THEIR WORK IN 1795

Sturdy old oak, branch lopped off over the Money Pit

Old ship's block and tackle, badly decayed

Saucer-shaped depression which first attracted attention

Layer of unusual, flat stones, unlike any others on Oak Island

Platforms of oak logs, firmly embedded

Soil subsidence: a foot or two below each oak platform

Refilled earth, comparatively easy to excavate

Pit sides of very hard, impermeable clay, showing pick marks from original excavation

Work abandoned at 30-foot platform

with some 'important work' in connection with farming, fishing or lumbering!

Daniel had judged his two young friends rightly: his contemporaries, John Smith and Anthony Vaughan, were as excited by the discovery as Daniel was, and accompanied him eagerly back to Oak Island equipped with mattocks and spades. A few minutes' work at the site told them that Daniel's first suspicions about the circular depression had been right.

The loose earth came out with surprising ease. What they were removing now was soil which had clearly been taken out before. Around the edges of the broad shaft which they were excavating, the boys saw the pick marks which had been left by whoever had dug there before them.

The lads noticed that the rotting block and tackle were fixed to the 'Y' shape formed between the ends of the lopped branch by means of an old wooden peg of the type described by shipbuilders of the time as a 'tree' or 'tree-nail.' This peg had apparently once formed a secure triangle in conjunction with the ends of the lopped bough.

Dr. Ogilvie's prodigious eight-volume *Imperial Dictionary*, which was published early in the nineteenth century, refers to various types of such shipbuilders' wooden pegs as 'chess-trees,' 'trestle-trees', 'cross-trees' and so on.

Had that lifting equipment been left by the original excavators of the Money Pit, or had some subsequent opportunist visitors to Oak Island — prior to Daniel and his friends in 1795 — seen the same circular depression and decided to excavate it with the aid of a block and tackle pegged to a convenient oak?

Two or three feet down the boys discovered a layer of flat stones, obviously placed there quite deliberately by someone who had been digging and refilling the pit before them. Their local knowledge told them that those stones could not have originated on Oak Island. The only similar ones, as far as they knew, were from the vicinity of Gold River, which lay roughly two miles north.

As Michael Bradley has pointed out in his painstakingly researched and superbly written *Holy Grail Across the Atlantic* (Toronto: Hounslow Press, 1988), there are two Oak Islands, one on each side of the peninsula. There are also two important rivers — each of which is adjacent to one of the Oak Islands. The southern Oak Island which contains the Money Pit is close to Gold River. The northern Oak Island (which ceased to be an island in the 1930s when dykes were built as part of a work programme during the Great Depression) is close to the Gaspareau River.

The name Gold River as a possible clue to the Oak

Island mystery is self-evident; but what of the name Gaspareau? Over the years a 'g' and a 'c' easily become interchangeable. *Cas* can mean a box or case, perhaps a treasure chest, or even a sarcophagus. *Cas* can mean a hut, a cabin, or even a square on a chess board — and chess boards figure very prominently in both Templar and Masonic symbolism. *Par* means with, or by, and *eau* is water. The *cas* could equally well have been *casse* meaning breakage or damage, or even cassette, a casket or money box. *Casque*, meaning helmet, is another strong possibility. This all reinforces Michael Bradley's intriguing argument that crossing the Atlantic, locating an island covered with non-indigenous oaks, and sailing up the river beside it would lead to a certain building, to a helmet (or to some honoured military leader who wore a helmet), to the square of destiny on life's metaphorical chessboard which the travellers were trying to reach, or to a sanctuary where that which was damaged could be restored, i.e., a place where an early sailing ship battered by the ordeal of an Atlantic crossing could be repaired and refitted.

Between the source of the Gaspareau River ('the-treasure-box-reached-by-water') and Gold River lie the mysterious and controversial ruins which the McKays showed to Michael Bradley. Perhaps something like a pentagonal, early medieval castle once stood there: there's enough left on the ground to be very interesting — but there's not quite enough to be absolutely certain about it.

Bradley's ingenious theories fit in well with the layer of Gold River stones which the young treasure hunters found near the top of the Money Pit.

There could be no surer indication that a connection had to be made between Gold River and Oak Island than to place a layer of Gold River stones over the highly significant pit. What could those stones have meant? Were they intended as a barrier, a "keep out" sign, to those who were initiated into some ancient mystery? Or were they intended to be something like a name plate on a door saying "Yes, you're right. This is the place. Dig here!" McGinnis,

Vaughan and Smith interpreted them as a sure indication that they were on to something very interesting indeed, and that pirates' gold, or some other great treasure, lay not far below.

When the human mind is set enthusiastically on one particular course, it gallops with the uncompromising directness of a blinkered horse: this is especially true when the chemistry of youth is effervescing vigorously and teenaged adrenalin is coursing through the veins. Those three lads would have had nothing on their minds except pirate treasure, and wonderful dreams of escaping from the back-breaking toil of farming, fishing and tree-felling. The last thing that would have occurred to them as they dug so eagerly was that they were up against one of the most cunningly constructed hiding places ever built, and that for the next two centuries the subtlety of the original designer would defeat the best efforts of modern engineering skill and technology.

Pirates deservedly acquired a reputation for ruthless greed and blood-thirsty viciousness, but not for industry. Pirates were traditionally careless, badly organised, lazy — and drunk most of the time. McGinnis and his friends did not expect the treasure they were looking for to be very deeply buried: six or seven feet down would be the most a pirate would dig. The layer of stones must have encouraged the lads to think that the chest of gold and jewels lay not much farther below. So they dug and they dug . . . and they found nothing.

Then, at last, ten feet below the surface, they hit a layer of tough old oak logs. This, they thought, had to be it. The ends of the logs were wedged securely into the firm clay of the pit's sides, although — like the ancient block and tackle — the wood itself was showing signs of decay on the surface. They prised the logs out with some difficulty, and saw that the soil below them had settled two or three feet — but there was still no sign of any chest or cask filled with pirates' gold and jewels. Tired and disappointed the boys dug on . . .

They got over some of their disappointment and frustration by reasoning among themselves that whatever was buried at this kind of depth had to be very valuable indeed. At the twenty-foot level they encountered another platform of oak logs, but still no gold.

At the thirty-foot level they found more oak logs — and very understandably decided that enough was enough. There was a limit to the amount of time which their families would allow them to spend away from the all important farming, fishing and lumbering on which their economic survival depended. Reluctantly, and with their dreams of wealth undiminished by their hard work and disappointment, the three boys marked the area carefully with wooden stakes, covered over the top of the pit with brushwood and branches and went back to their normal daily routines.

As time passed John built a house near the pit and managed to acquire plots fifteen to twenty, thus becoming the owner of the whole twenty-four acres at the eastern end of the island. The original little settlement town of Shoreham eventually grew into the modern fishing village of Chester. The Shoreham Grant contained approximately one hundred thousand acres (roughly forty-one thousand hectares) in all, and the 128 acres of Oak Island were a very small fraction of the total involved. Records show, however, that in 1759 Oak Island was owned by former New England families named Young, Lynch, Seacombe and Monro. It is highly probable that our good friend and very knowledgeable Oak Island informant, George Young, a recently retired Nova Scotian surveyor, is related to that same Young family who were part owners of Oak Island under that original Shoreham Grant.

The earliest existing deed showing a change of land ownership on Oak Island indicates that Timothy Lynch bought plot nineteen from Edward Smith on March 8, 1768. Both men lived in Chester, and the plot was sold for five pounds sterling.

It seems likely that it was Edward Smith who sold his land to Timothy Lynch who gave his name to Smith's Cove.

The two Smiths don't seem to have been related, as early records suggest that the John Smith who later bought the eastern end of Oak Island had originally come from Boston and had been in Nova Scotia only since 1790.

With stakes to mark the place, brushwood over the top of the pit and John Smith in legal possession of the plot which contained it, the first attempt to get at the treasure ended. No one else, it seemed, was willing to put time or money into helping the three young adventurers who had made their great discovery in 1795. It was not only pressure of work which discouraged the local settlers from getting involved with Oak Island. The place had a sinister reputation. Oak Island was, in many local minds a place of ill omen.

It was by no means unusual for pirates to bury a watchman with their treasure, so that his aggrieved and restless spirit would act as a vengeful, supernatural guardian of their hidden wealth. There are also curious legends of a great black dog having been seen on the island from time to time.

This links up with various legends of hell hounds from many ages and many lands. Most of those legends can be traced back to Cerberus, the three-headed dog of Roman mythology who was believed to guard the entrance to the underworld. Hercules succeeded in dragging the monster up to earth, and then let him go again. Orpheus lulled him to sleep by playing his lyre. The Sibyl who conducted Aeneas through the underworld put Cerberus to sleep with a cake made from poppies and honey. Brewer's famous *Dictionary of Phrase and Fable* suggests that the Cerberus myth arose from the ancient Egyptian custom of using fierce dogs to guard graves from would-be thieves and desecrators.

In our own native Norfolk in England, we are familiar with very persistent legends of the Black Shuck, a ghostly dog who is said to haunt the north Norfolk coast, travelling between the graves of two brothers who once owned him but were drowned at sea. Their bodies were washed ashore and buried in different village churchyards; the faithful hound spends one night on each grave in turn. A far less sentimental East Anglian legend is the story of the Black Dog of Bungay — described as the size of a pony and with eyes like live coals. This monster was said to have broken into Bungay Church one night and savaged many of the worshippers. Another explanation for these supernatural hound stories is the legend of the Wild Hunt.

There is an ancient German version of this legend concerning the Black Forest, and a French version involving the woods at Fountainebleau. The English tale concerns Herne the Hunter who is associated with Herne's Oak and Windsor Forest. All these wild spectral huntsmen were accompanied by their hounds.

If, as Michael Bradley thoughtfully suggests, there is strong evidence that the Oak Island treasure has a medieval European connection, then it is not beyond the bounds of possibility that the Oak Island Hound story is connected with one of the wild hunt legends. Herne, it must also be remembered, was strongly associated with oak trees, as were the ancient Druids. If a medieval Wild Hunt legend filtered across to Oak Island, was it carried there by medieval voyagers?

The search for the treasure was in abeyance for a year or two, and then John Smith had a momentous meeting with Simeon Lynds.

3

THE WORK OF THE ONSLOW COMPANY IN 1803

The next adventurer to take up the challenge of Oak Island was Simeon Lynds, although there is some confusion about how he came to be involved. One version relates that he was a doctor from Truro, Nova Scotia, who attended the birth of Mrs Smith's first child in 1802. According to this account, while they were waiting for the baby to arrive John told Dr Lynds about the Money Pit, and the unsuccessful attempts which he, Daniel and Anthony had made seven or eight years previously. Records appear to indicate, however, that the Smiths' first child had already been baptised in 1798.

Another more widely known and more likely version makes Simeon Lynds a local businessman from either Truro or nearby Onslow, who was a friend, or relative, of Anthony Vaughan's or John Smith's father — possibly of both men. On a visit to Vaughan or Smith, senior, Lynds heard about the boys' adventures in 1795, went over to the island with them to look around and came away convinced. The third version places Lynds as a business visitor to Chester who met Anthony Vaughan there and heard the Money Pit story from him. An article from *The Colonist* dated January 2, 1864, refers to 'the late Simeon Lynds' as a relative of Vaughan's father, who was let into the Money Pit secret because of his family ties with the Vaughans.

This *Colonist* source also suggests that it was Simeon's father, Thomas Lynds, who had the money and the right social connections to get the Onslow Company launched.

Relative, doctor, family friend, or travelling businessman, Simeon Lynds was intrigued by the account he had heard. He, or his father, certainly organised an effective consortium of business and professional men in and around Onslow, which became known as The Onslow Company. One member was Sheriff Tom Harris, another was Colonel Archibald, a town clerk and justice of the peace. He may well have been the father, or grandfather, of the other Archibald who was involved some fifty years later in the Pitblado episode.

The Onslow men dug away steadily, unearthing platforms of oak logs at regular ten-foot intervals as they cleared out more and more of the pit, but they encountered other curious layers as well. There are minor discrepancies and divergences in the accounts of what precisely was discovered at which level, but as the digging continued layers of putty, charcoal and coconut fibre were pulled out.

There was so much putty spread over one layer of oak logs, according to one account, that it was used to glaze the windows of more than twenty local houses.

Hiram Walker was a ship's carpenter who lived in Chester at the time, and worked on the Money Pit. Years later he told his granddaughter, Mrs Cottnam Smith, that he had seen 'bushels of coconut fibre' being lifted out of the shaft as the work progressed.

These points about the quantities of putty and coconut fibre are significant ones. Those earlier investigators who have tried to suggest that the Money Pit was merely a natural sink-hole in the limestone, and that the tunnels connecting it to Smith's Cove and the southern shore were just fortuitous faults in the rock, have argued that the oak logs, fibre, putty and charcoal had either slid into the shaft over many years, or been carried in up the tunnels gradually by the tides of centuries.

The actual descriptions of the pit and the accounts of

how the work proceeded tell very different stories. A little coconut fibre might have drifted in, a few kilograms of putty might have been washed ashore from a wreck, a chunk or two of charcoal from a camp fire, or a burnt out vessel might have got down a natural shaft. The imagination can even stretch to a few oak branches blowing down in a gale and sliding together like a 'platform' down the natural sink-hole.

One 'oak platform'? One or two nuggets of marine putty? A handful of charcoal? A few yards' drift of sparsely distributed coconut fibre? That much might just have got down there naturally. But there were at least ten oak platforms, at regular intervals, all wedged firmly into the hard clay of the shaft's walls. There was a full, flat, regular layer of charcoal, and a similar one of putty. There was enough coconut fibre to fill several bushel baskets. But the most damning pieces of contradictory evidence were the original diggers' pick marks clearly visible in the hard clay walls in 1795.

Another very intriguing find for the Onslow Company was the large flat stone encountered just above the ninety-foot level.

The diggers tried to decipher the coded message but without success, wondering whether it was a vital clue to the whereabouts of the treasure, or to the identity of the original miners.

Almost as great a mystery as the strange inscription is the curious riddle of what subsequently happened to the stone itself. John Smith was halfway through building a fireplace in his Oak Island farmhouse: he incorporated the stone into that — partly to keep it safe, and partly to provide a conversation piece.

In 1865 the stone was taken from the Smith homestead and placed on display in the window of the bookbindery belonging to A. and H. Creighton in Halifax. A.O. Creighton was at that time treasurer of one of the Oak Island treasure hunting syndicates, and it was hoped that the displayed stone would encourage new shareholders to

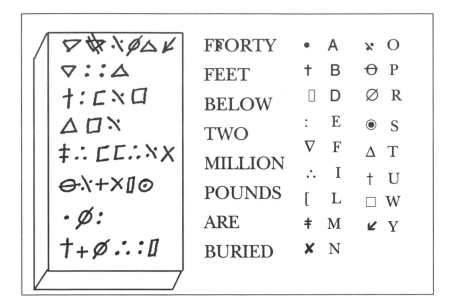

participate in the search. A witness named Jefferson MacDonald is reported to have said that he had seen the stone at close quarters, had helped to move it in fact, and that there was no doubt at all that there was a coded inscription on it which no-one had been able to solve.

A.O. Creighton left the business in 1879 and a new firm was started by Herbert Creighton and Edward Marshall. Edward's son Harry was with the firm from 1890 onwards and he made a statement about the stone in 1935 to treasure hunter Frederick Blair and his lawyer Reginald Harris. The gist of Harry Marshall's evidence was that he remembered the stone well, but had never seen the inscription on it because it had been worn away by years of use as a bookbinder's beating stone. He said that the stone was two feet long, just over a foot wide and about ten inches thick. He guessed its weight in the region of 175 pounds[3]. Both surfaces were smooth, but the sides were rough. Harry

---

[3]Something doesn't quite seem to click here. If these dimensions and the weight are taken as accurate, the density of the stone can be calculated to be 1.68. This is rather light considering that most of the minerals of the earth's crust have densities between 2.8 and 3.5. Could the stone possibly have been *hollow*?

added that it was a very hard, finely grained stone with an olive tinge. He thought it might have been porphyry or granite. He also commented that it was totally unlike any stone he had ever seen in Nova Scotia.

If Harry Marshall was correct in his guess that the strange stone was porphyry, then a link with ancient Egypt may be established. In the days of Pliny (first century A.D.) mottled red or purple rocks were called porphorytes from the Greek word meaning 'red.' Much of this early stone was volcanic, but the first Italian sculptors thought it was a variety of marble. The best red porphyry, known as *porfido rosso antico*, from which many ancient Egyptian monuments were carved, came from substantial deposits along the west coast of the Red Sea. The secret of its whereabouts was lost for many years, but the quarry was rediscovered at Jebel Dhokan.

Edward R. Snow mentions the stone in *True Tales of Buried Treasure* (New York: Dodd, Mead and Co., 1962) and relates that the Reverend A.T. Kempton of Cambridge, Massachusetts, said that an old Irish teacher had translated it to read: "Forty feet below two million pounds are buried." Our own cryptographer, computer engineer Paul V.S. Townsend, M.Sc., reached the same conclusion independently in under ten minutes. The decipherment is shown in the illustration on the previous page, along with the key to the symbols used. The second character is assumed to be a second point-down triangle (F) drawn in error and crossed out — this character is ignored in the decoding.

All very well, but everything depends upon whether the inscription as recorded is the original one which actually appeared on the stone when it was first unearthed from the Money Pit in 1803. The suspicion lingers that someone anxious to raise funds in 1865 put an entirely spurious message on the stone using a simple substitution cipher that was easy to crack. Conan Doyle's short story *The Dancing Men* provides a similar riddle for Holmes to solve. What if that easy hoax code overlaid a genuine ancient inscription of similar appearance, to which the hoaxer had only to make a few additions and alterations? In that case we are dealing with a stone palimpsest, something from which the original writing has been erased or covered to make way for further writing. Historically, the process was usually applied to parchments and monumental brasses which were turned and re-engraved on the reverse side. The original Greek words *palin* and *psao* from which 'palimpsest' is derived mean literally 'again' and 'to rub smooth.'

George Young drew our attention to a decipherment of the stone made by Professor Barry Fell from a copy of the inscription provided for him by Phyllis Donohue. Fell, an internationally acclaimed epigrapher, produced a religious text translation of the Money Pit stone from an early Libyan Arabic dialect used by a branch of the North African Coptic Church centuries ago.

Coptic is best understood as the linguistic descendant of the ancient Egyptian language. The oldest documents in Coptic date back to the second and third centuries of the Christian era and are translations of the Christian scriptures. The writers tended to use Greek with seven demotic symbols added, rather than to use their own demotic script.

Coptic is known to exist in six forms: Bashmuric and Bohairic from Lower Egypt; Fayumic, Asyutic, Akhmimic and Sahidic from Upper Egypt. There may be others.

What is of particular interest about a probable Coptic inscription on the Money Pit stone, and its relevance to the final solution of the Oak Island mystery, is that two very early Coptic manuscripts, the *Pistis Sophia* in the British Museum and the *Bruce Codex* in the Bodleian Library, both relate to an obscure Gnostic sect operating in Egypt in the third century A.D. Ancient Gnostic secrets are inextricably interwoven into the mystery of Rennes-le-Château, and the Rennes clues in turn throw light on the Oak Island problem.

If George Young's thought-provoking hypothesis and Professor Fell's scholarly interpretation are the correct ones — and there is some real likelihood that they are —

then they provide an intriguing link between ancient Egypt and Oak Island.

James McNutt, who was working on Oak Island in the 1860s, refers to the inscribed slab as a piece of 'freestone' and said that it was unlike any other stone on the Nova Scotian coast. Towards the close of the nineteenth century, Judge Des Brisays wrote an authoritative account of the Oak Island events up to and including his own time. He refers to the stone and says that the finders were unable to make sense of it '. . . either because it was too badly cut, or did not appear to be in their own vernacular . . .'

So the Onslow team has removed the curiously coded slab and resumed excavations. We can picture them now at the ninety-foot level. The daylight is fading as they remove the oak platform which lay just below the stone slab. One after another the men begin to notice that water is leaking into the Money Pit — and in substantial quantities. By this time they are taking out one load of water for every two loads of clay.

Convinced that the mysterious stone meant something, and that they must now be very close to whatever precious object was buried in the shaft, they began probing the soggy base of the pit with long iron rods. At the ninety-eight-foot level those probes struck something impenetrably hard which extended from one side of the Money Pit to the other. Water and darkness were now posing such serious problems that the Onslow men decided to resume their search at first light: it turned out to be a life-saving decision.

First light brought a grim disappointment: the Money Pit was over sixty feet deep in water. One account relates that as they gathered round the opening, an unlucky member of the expedition slipped into the flooded shaft, only to splutter to the surface shouting that the water tasted of salt. "Salt!" he repeated, as his companions lowered a rope and hauled him to safety. The implication was that in some inexplicable way the Atlantic had found its way through the hitherto impenetrable clay. It did not dawn on the Onslow men at that stage that the ocean might have had some help from the original architect of the Money Pit and its bewildering labyrinth.

Doggedly, they began trying to empty the pit by bailing it like a leaking ship, but this had no effect whatsoever — they were merely redistributing the Atlantic Ocean!

It was now time to attend to harvest and other duties back home, so work ended for 1803, but the following year the Onslow Company was back as determined as ever. This time they planned to dig a parallel shaft fifteen feet southeast of the Money Pit itself and then tunnel across to reach the treasure. Their parallel shaft reached 115 feet without encountering any water problems at all. Optimistically, the tunnellers began to cut horizontally through the stubborn clay towards the Money Pit itself. They accomplished the first twelve or thirteen feet without any serious problems: less than three feet now separated the excited miners from the spot where they believed the treasure lay.

Water started seeping through again, slowly at first, then in small streams. The clay between their tunnel end and the Money Pit collapsed: they were very lucky to escape without loss of life. In just over an hour the second shaft was over sixty feet deep in salt water. Remembering all too well how hopeless bailing had been last time, they made a brief, half-hearted attempt to empty their new shaft, but again their buckets had not the slightest effect on the flood water. They were strong, determined men, but they recognised that this project was totally beyond their resources. Harvests had to be gathered; land had to be tilled; fish had to be caught and timber had to be felled if the colonists and their families were to live. The Onslow Company gave up and returned to their farms, their stores and their fishing boats.

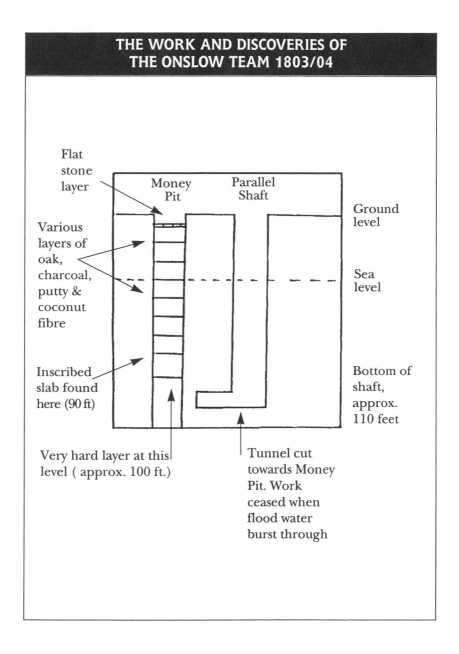

THE WORK AND DISCOVERIES OF
THE ONSLOW TEAM 1803/04

Flat stone layer

Money Pit

Parallel Shaft

Ground level

Various layers of oak, charcoal, putty & coconut fibre

Sea level

Inscribed slab found here (90 ft)

Bottom of shaft, approx. 110 feet

Very hard layer at this level (approx. 100 ft.)

Tunnel cut towards Money Pit. Work ceased when flood water burst through

4

THE TRURO COMPANY'S ATTEMPT IN 1849

Daniel McGinnis was already in his grave and Smith and Vaughan were both in their seventies before the next attack on the Money Pit was launched. This was undertaken by the Truro Company in 1849. The mysterious treasure which John and Anthony had been trying to locate since they were teenagers remained as tantalising and as elusive as ever.

Some accounts list the members of the Truro Syndicate as including a Dr David Barnes Lynds, who may have been Simeon's son or grandson. Other accounts relate that it was Simeon himself, now a very old man, who was the Lynds involved with the Truro Syndicate of 1849. It is not beyond the bounds of possibility. Captain Anthony Vaughan, either the son or grandson of the Anthony Vaughan who made the original discovery, died in New York in 1948 at the age of 100. This same Captain Vaughan remembered how as a very young boy he had been present when a major discovery — a set of fan shaped drains — had been made at Smith's Cove. It was the Truro Syndicate who found both these beach drains and at least one of the flood tunnels which linked them to the Money Pit. In addition to whichever Lynds it was, plus Smith and Vaughan, the aging survivors of the 1795 discovery, the Truro group, which was formally inaugurated in 1845, consisted of John (or James) Pitblado (or Pitbladdo), John Gamell, Robert Creelman, Adam Tupper and Jotham McCully. McCully was their site manager in charge of all operations. Pitblado was responsible for drilling and ancillary activities. Their work on the island began in earnest in 1849. The invaluable continuity provided by the presence of earlier searchers like Smith and Vaughan gave the Truro team a flying start.

Forty years had gone by since the Onslow men's heroic failure, and during those four decades the original Money Pit, along with the drainage shafts which had been dug nearby, had collapsed. Old Anthony Vaughan was still able to identify the site of the original Money Pit with perfect accuracy and the Truro workers began re-excavating there. Just a few feet down they found the remains of a broken pump which the Onslow men had abandoned when their work was overwhelmed by flood water.

Hoping that the inundation which had beaten the Onslow syndicate so long ago had now subsided, the Truro team continued excavating ever deeper. They were well over eighty feet down after some two weeks' digging and their luck was still holding as far as the water was concerned.

It was a Saturday night. Sunday was an important holy day to pious nineteenth century Nova Scotians — even if they did believe that a fabulous treasure lay scarcely ten feet farther down the shaft they were re-excavating. The pit looked dry and safe: all the signs were favourable as the Truro men went off to worship in Chester that Sunday morning.

When they returned to Oak Island after lunch the Money Pit was sixty feet deep in water — exactly as it had been when it bested the Onslow men in 1805. They bailed as vigorously as their Onslow predecessors had done, but it had no perceptible effect on the water level. One eye-witness said that it was like trying to eat soup with a fork!

Jotham McCully believed in the prudent old military maxim: "Time spent in reconnaissance is never wasted." He decided to explore the depths of the shaft with a pod auger.

This was a piece of prospecting equipment mainly used in the mid-nineteenth century by mining speculators looking for coal. The key to its operation was a vital component known as a 'valve sludger'. This was a sturdy tube for raising the core samples: it worked on the principle of a one way valve which would pick up material, as it cut its way downwards. The Truro men's tragedy was their need to economise on equipment: they had only one valve sludger and they lost it about 110 feet down while drilling their first exploratory hole. A pod auger has a strong, sharp tip (rather like a chisel) and spiral grooves similar to those in a rifle barrel for retrieving the core samples.

The only replacement for the valve sludger available to them was of very inferior design: it had a simple ball and retaining pin instead of a proper valve. The pin not only prevented the ball from dropping out: it prevented most small, loose objects such as coins or jewels from being retrieved. Soil, clay, rock splinters, wood or fibre fragments could circumnavigate the pin — pieces of treasure could not. This small, but vitally important, difference in the augers was the cause of the Truro syndicate's subsequent frustration and disappointment. Their pod auger went right through two buried casks or boxes of loose metal without being able to bring any of the contents to the surface.

To try to maximise the effectiveness of their drill the Truro team constructed a sturdy working platform thirty feet down the Money Pit just above the flood water. From this vantage point they made their first hole slightly west of centre. It was this hole which cost them their valve sludger. The remaining holes were in a line which moved east from the initial boring. The first two sets of samples produced only mud, clay, soil, gravel and a few insignificant stones which were small enough to negotiate the retaining pin below the ball. The next three holes provided important evidence.

At the ninety-eight foot level — precisely at the depth where the Onslow men had hit it with their iron probing rods forty years earlier — the pod auger went through a spruce platform nearly six inches thick. There was then a space of a foot or so through which the bit dropped effortlessly. Below this small empty zone, the auger bit through four inches of oak and then encountered nearly two feet of tantalising loose metal which it could not retrieve. Next came a further four inches of oak, which was immediately repeated. The auger then threaded its way awkwardly and reluctantly through another two feet or so of the irretrievable loose metal. After that it chopped through another four inches of oak with six inches of spruce below that. Under this spruce layer the auger detected seven or eight feet of backfilled clay, which had evidently been disturbed at some time in the past. Below this previously worked material the drill encountered only natural virgin clay as far as McCully and his men could ascertain.

Subsequent drillings again hit the ninety-eight-foot platform and the side of a chest, cask or sarcophagus. Small splinters of wood came up from it, and McCully noted with commendable precision and attention to detail that the drill behaved oddly and erratically as though the revolving chisel tip was struck repeatedly against a wooden obstruction parallel to one side of the descending drill. Coconut fibre also came up, and, very significantly, three or four links of gold chain: perhaps from a necklace or bracelet; perhaps from the epaulette of an officer's uniform, or from the ornately decorated robes of a long dead religious leader. McCully himself wondered if it was part of an old-fashioned watch chain.

The continuity and interconnection of the various teams who worked on the Money Pit are significant. Two of the original Onslow men in 1803 had been Colonel Robert Archibald and Captain David Archibald. In 1849, Pitblado certainly knew Charles Dickson Archibald of the Acadian Iron Works. This was located in Londonderry, Nova Scotia. James (or John?) Pitblado may have been a somewhat dubious character, or, at the most charitable interpretation, an unscrupulous opportunist. He had been instructed by the Truro team to bring every fragment raised by the drill for microscopic examination. John Gammell, a major shareholder, claimed that he had seen Pitblado take something from the drill, examine it very closely and slip it into his pocket surreptitiously when he thought he was unobserved. Gammell challenged Pitblado and asked to see what had been retrieved. Pitblado refused, saying he would show it to all the shareholders together at their next meeting. He never did. Leaving the island that day with the mystery object, Pitblado contacted Charles Archibald, who applied for a Government licence to search for treasure on Oak Island. All he got were the rights to hunt on empty land, or

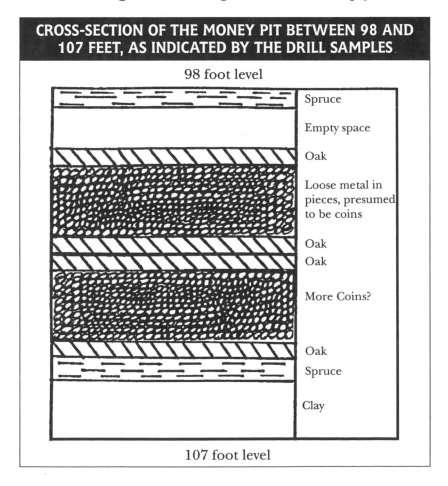

CROSS-SECTION OF THE MONEY PIT BETWEEN 98 AND 107 FEET, AS INDICATED BY THE DRILL SAMPLES.

98 foot level

Spruce

Empty space

Oak

Loose metal in pieces, presumed to be coins

Oak
Oak

More Coins?

Oak
Spruce

Clay

107 foot level

land which had not been granted to anyone. Not satisfied with that — it excluded him and Pitblado from the vital Money Pit area — he attempted to buy the east end of Oak Island. He failed. Not long afterwards he left Nova Scotia and settled in England. Pitblado vanished into obscurity amid contradictory hearsay. Some reports made him the first victim of the legendary Oak Island nemesis. One account says he was killed in a mining accident; another relates that it happened during railroad construction. Whatever the precise circumstances of his death, word went round that Pitblado had died shortly after pocketing that unknown fragment of treasure which he had found in the pod auger. What might that mysterious object have been? The first suggestion is that it was a small piece of gold, or a jewel. It might also have been a scrap of parchment, a precursor of the tiny piece which was retrieved by T.P. Putnam and examined by Dr Andrew Porter on September 6, 1897. Another intriguing possibility is that Pitblado found not merely a precious jewel or gemstone, but one which bore a carefully inscribed Mason's Mark. Suppose that the inscription on the strange stone unearthed by the Onslow men had contained Masons' Marks and that these had been regarded as an unknown alphabet by the men who had puzzled over them in 1803.

Pitblado's action has yet another parallel with the curious story of Rennes-le-Château: according to one account, during the restoration work on the church, in the course of which the "Knight's Tombstone" was discovered, one of the builders thought he saw something glinting underneath. Saunière abruptly brought the day's work to a halt on the grounds that they could not leave a hole in the floor on the Sunday following. By the time work resumed on Monday, somebody had disturbed the stone which had been left covering the hole, and the "glinting object" had disappeared.

Back to the Truro team on Oak Island! The explorers next made a discovery that diverted their attention from Pitblado's disloyalty. They noticed that the water in the flooded shafts rose and fell a foot or two as the tides came and went around the island. The question that McCully and his team asked themselves repeatedly was: "Why was there no water in any of the additional shafts until those shafts were connected to the Money Pit?" The clay was very hard, practically impermeable. Few men knew better than those rugged old Truro diggers just how hard the going really was. They argued that if a natural waterway or underground stream ran from deep in the Money Pit to the Atlantic Ocean it would have prevented the original workers from completing their design. In addition, the impermeable clay through which the shaft had been sunk made such a natural watercourse very improbable.

Observations at Smith's Cove at low tide had revealed water trickling down the beach towards the sea. Putting their observations and deductions together, the Truro men began to wonder whether the unknown miners who had sunk the Money Pit with its many elaborate layers of oak, putty, fibre and charcoal, had somehow connected it to the ocean.

The Truro team began to dig up the beach at Smith's Cove. The first thing they found was a massive sheet of coconut fibre which covered the shore line for about 150 feet. The fibre layer was between two and three inches deep and below it lay several more inches of tough, old, salt-resistant eel grass, which was, however, now showing signs of decay. It had evidently been there a long time. This double blanket of eel grass and coconut fibre covered the shore between high and low tide levels. It would seem to have served two purposes: to retain and transmit water like an enormous sponge; and to prevent sand and clay from passing through to clog whatever lay beneath.

Simplicity is the hallmark of genius. Standing on the shoulders of the intellectual giants who pioneered the path, the average man and woman can see their way forward to new discoveries. Armed with high-powered computers linked to I.T. databases, third year high school students can solve in minutes problems that would have delayed Archimedes, Newton or Einstein for several weeks. To construct an underground defence system using twentieth century technology, high-powered excavators and bulldozers is no more than an average task: to construct it with very simple and limited resources is an outstanding achievement.

Under the eel grass and coconut fibre filter-blanket, the Unknown Engineer laid a mass of stones and boulders completely free from sand and clay. It seemed to bear a remarkable similarity to a Roman road, as if its builder had been familiar with their road-building technique.

Jotham McCully's keen eyes noted the remains of an old coffer dam surrounding these amazing beach workings. If that was how the original builders had done it, his men could do it too. Accordingly, the Truro team built their own coffer dam around the zone they were investigating.

With the sea water out of the way, they dug down below

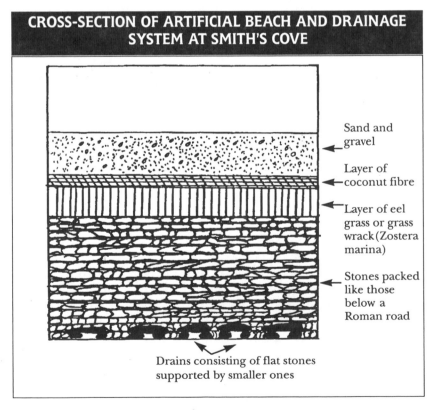

CROSS-SECTION OF ARTIFICIAL BEACH AND DRAINAGE SYSTEM AT SMITH'S COVE

Sand and gravel

Layer of coconut fibre

Layer of eel grass or grass wrack (Zostera marina)

Stones packed like those below a Roman road

Drains consisting of flat stones supported by smaller ones

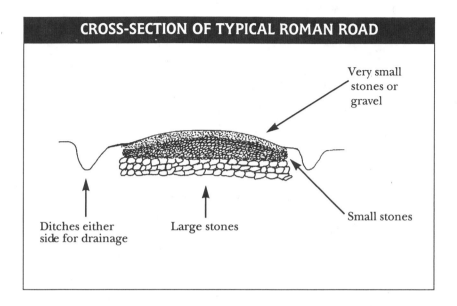

CROSS-SECTION OF TYPICAL ROMAN ROAD

Very small stones or gravel

Small stones

Ditches either side for drainage

Large stones

the stones and discovered a set of five fan-shaped box drains relentlessly conducting the Atlantic into the lower levels of the Money Pit.

With their quickly erected and non-too-sturdy coffer dam in place, the Truro men began to trace the drainage system back up the beach as it converged on the main flood tunnel leading to the Money Pit. About fifteen or twenty yards along they were having to dig down four or five feet to locate the drains.

Disaster struck in the form of an abnormally high tide which overflowed their temporary coffer dam. It was constructed to take pressure from the Atlantic side, but not from a weight of inshore water trying to flow back down the beach: it broke and was washed away. The Truro team was beginning to suffer from two of the major frustrations experienced by almost all Oak Island teams sooner or later: insufficient time and insufficient funds.

On balance, McCully and the shareholders decided that trying to rebuild the dam would not be cost effective. What they had already been able to study of the artificial beach with its drainage system and filter-blankets had given them a fair idea of where the flood tunnel would run.

They decided to try to intercept and block that main tunnel itself rather than to attempt any further work on the artificial beach at Smith's Cove. Drawing a line from the point where the beach drains seemed to converge back to the Money Pit itself, they selected a likely looking point on that line and began to dig. The expected course of events was as shown in the upper diagram: the interceptor shaft would meet the flood tunnel at a depth considerably less than the presumed junction with the Money Pit at 110 feet, after which the lower course of the flood tunnel could be blocked.

Thirty, forty, fifty feet: the interceptor shaft cut deeper and deeper. Just short of eighty feet, they gave up: it couldn't be this deep and still connect with the ninety-five-foot level, or could it?

It did not seem to have occurred to the Truro team that the cunning artificer against whom they were pitting their wits might just have decided to take his flood tunnel deeper than anyone would dig to intercept it, and then allow the natural hydraulic forces to push the water up again to the critical ninety-foot level in the Money Pit, as shown in the lower diagram.

Rightly or wrongly, the Truro men began digging a second interceptor tunnel ten or twelve feet south of their seventy-five-foot failure. Between thirty and forty feet down in this new shaft they hit a substantial boulder. Prizing it out with considerable difficulty, they were deluged with water: they had found at least one of the flood tunnels, or, perhaps, an upper branch of a flood tunnel. As the diggers scrambled out of their newly dug interceptor shaft, salt water welled up rapidly until it reached sea level. Whatever passageway that boulder had been covering, it undoubtedly connected with the Atlantic.

Working with considerable difficulty, they did what they could to staunch the flow by driving heavy wooden stakes down into the base of their shaft and attempting to block the tunnel with clay. It was only a partial success. When

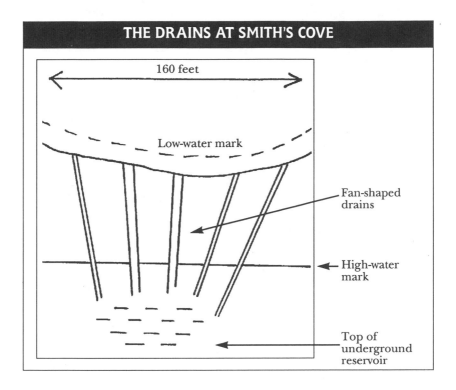

THE DRAINS AT SMITH'S COVE

160 feet

Low-water mark

Fan-shaped drains

High-water mark

Top of underground reservoir

they began trying to bail out the Money Pit again they lowered the level a little, but nowhere near enough to make further excavation possible.

Not really knowing what to try next, they resorted to the old formula of a parallel shaft either to drain the Money Pit or to make it possible to tunnel across to remove the treasure horizontally. Predictably, this re-run of previous failures led to yet another ignominious retreat up yet another flooded shaft.

This was the ironic end of the Truro team's endeavours: no more capital could be raised just when the explorers were more convinced than ever that a vast treasure lay in the depths of the Money Pit: inaccessible — yet tantalisingly close.

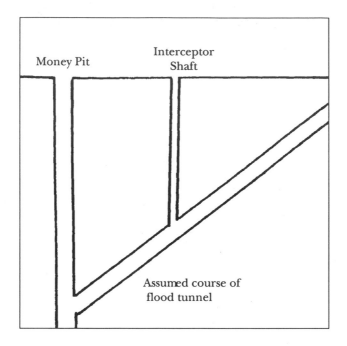

Money Pit

Interceptor
Shaft

Assumed course of
flood tunnel

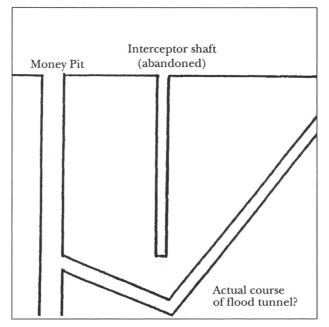

Money Pit

Interceptor shaft
(abandoned)

Actual course
of flood tunnel?

5

THE DRAIN AND TUNNEL SYSTEM

Jotham B. McCully and his Truro men had discovered the amazing drainage system and the artificial beach at Smith's Cove. It partly answered the question of how water was reaching the Money Pit below the ninety-foot level, but it raised many more questions than it answered.

Looked at as a problem in basic logistics, there is: the construction of the coffer dam; the removal of the natural sand and clay from that area; the location, transportation and embedding of the stones and boulders; the planning and laying of the five fan-shaped drains; the digging of at least one — possibly two or three — flood tunnels; and the accurate connection of the tunnel, or tunnels, to the Money Pit at depths greater than ninety feet. By calculating the size of the coffer dam; the area and depth of the artificial beach; the amount of clay which would have had to be removed from the tunnel and dumped elsewhere . . . and various other factors, a broad idea of the number of man-hours could be estimated.

Some types of work are totally flexible in their homogeneity and their consequent man-hour implications. For example, some jobs can be done equally well by one man taking eighty hours, by ten men taking eight hours or by 160 men taking half-an-hour. Other tasks have specific requirements which make team work more effective than individual work. Some work theatres' physical and spatial limitations make large teams impractical.

Only one or two men at a time can cut away at the same narrow seam face in certain mines, for example. Other occupations need forty or fifty powerful workers operating simultaneously to raise a heavy mast, or to haul a ship up a beach to be careened. A work-study expert could devise an optimum number of workers for each of the various sub-tasks involved in creating the Money Pit and its ancillary drainage and tunnel systems. Experts might reach marginally different conclusions, but they would be in broad agreement about the size of the work force required to complete the whole job in a reasonable time. Unless we are prepared to consider a project that would stretch into years rather than months, we must envisage a work force of at least thirty people, with the necessary picks, shovels, ropes, pulleys, trolleys, sledges, barrels and carts to make the job possible.

At the back of all this physical effort there has to be inspired planning: careful, accurate designing and effective administration and organisation. The Oak Island engineers and miners needed food, drink, clothing and shelter — not just for basic humanitarian reasons, but simply to keep them functioning effectively. The least caring slave exploiter provided the minimal conditions necessary to keep his slaves working. It was enlightened self-interest.

To try to understand the Oak Island Money Pit mystery, the investigator must attempt to answer these questions in connection with the artificial beach, the drains, the filters and the flood tunnels:

(a) Who had the engineering and administrative skills to plan and organise all of this?

(b) Who had the necessary work force available: voluntary, coerced, enslaved, or otherwise?

(c) Who had the time to keep that workforce on site for several months while the huge task was completed?

(d) Who had the essential resources and equipment available to feed and supply that substantial work force for the duration of the original Money Pit construction work?

(e) Who had the necessary motivation to initiate the whole amazing project in the first place, and the stamina to see it through to a satisfactory conclusion?

(f) Who believed that the contents of the Money Pit, the mysterious "x" which the pit and its flood system was built to protect, was really worth all that time, effort, planning and organisation?

Taking point (a) first, the possessor of the necessary engineering and administrative skills could have been a naval or military officer, especially one whose speciality was attacking or defending fortified positions, and, most appropriate of all, an engineering officer. Someone with tin, gold or silver mining experience, perhaps in the old flood-prone tin mines of Cornwall, would be another likely candidate. A character from one of the famous Poldark historical romances springs to mind. Lower down the list, but by no means out of the running, might well be a Master Mason with Templar connections, a Viking boat builder, a Celtic sea-rover with experience of Welsh gold-mining, a Coptic religious refugee with experience of Egyptian building and tunnelling techniques, or a Mayan or Aztec architect.

Which of these candidates would have been most likely to have had factor (b), a large and well disciplined work force, available? A detachment of sailors or marines, perhaps? Drake's dedicated Devonshire men, reinforced by a handful of Cornish tin miners, would readily have exchanged the hazards of the Spanish Main for the perils of the deep shafts and galleries ashore.

Discipline and order were the very essence of masonic life and the strict Rule of the Knights Templar. Masons and Templars would have worked unquestioningly and uncomplainingly at their Master's bidding to construct the Oak Island system. The Mores, with their proud and ruthless Viking Norman ancestry, eventually became the noble Sinclairs, the followers of the "Holy Light," the Sanctus

Clarus. Never lacking in courage, nor in building skills, a party of loyal Norsemen could have worked solidly together to construct the Money Pit and its defences. Celtic sea-rovers from Wales or Ireland would have had that fierce loyalty to their tribal chief which would have inspired them to sink the great shaft on Oak Island at his command — or to protect his corpse.

Or was George Young right in following Professor Fell's erudite translation of the words on that mysterious porphyry tablet discovered in 1803? Were the original builders a group of Coptic Christian refugees from Egypt who had made a semi-miraculous journey through the Pillars of Hercules and across the Atlantic in their resilient papyrus boats? Men schooled in the ancient skills and traditions of the pyramid builders would have had little trouble in digging out the shafts and tunnels of Oak Island.

An ardently religious fellowship would have provided an ideally dedicated and devoted labour force to carry out the work. The Mayan and Aztec socio-political systems would also have provided bands of disciplined workers able and willing to undertake whatever arduous tasks their Priests and Kings laid upon them. The Oak Island structures would not have been beyond the competence of those old South American architects and their docile labourers.

Possible leaders and suitable work forces abound: but who would have had the (c) factor — time? Although best equipped, an eighteenth century military or naval group under tactical or strategic pressure might have had least time in which to complete the huge undertaking. The same strictures would have applied to Drake's Devonshire men two centuries before. Time was of the essence for Elizabethan maritime adventurers: an undertaking that could have been accomplished much faster than the Oak Island structure would have had more appeal for Drake and his men.

Master Masons and Templars, however, would not have been in a hurry. Turning their broad backs on an ungrateful Europe following the treachery of the odious Philip IV in

1307, the remnants of the Templars were nurtured and protected by the valiant Scottish Sinclairs. With that Sinclair help, a Templar expedition might well have reached Nova Scotia and set up an elaborate headquarters and secret treasure store on Oak Island long before Columbus sailed.

Refugees do not lack time. The patient strength which fashioned the great Templar fortresses of the Middle East could well have been applied to the long, slow process of securing their priceless treasures in the depths of the Money Pit and guarding it with a prodigious system of beach drains and flood tunnels.

Viking and Celtic sea raiders were often characterised by the speed with which they attacked and sailed away again. The laboriously slow Money Pit work is not really their style, but there are exceptions. To honour a dead leader, Vikings have been known to bury their hero and his ship together: the Money Pit would scarcely be more time-consuming than a ship burial. If, as George Young suspects, there are coffins rather than treasure chests down there, then a Viking origin is not entirely impossible.

Mayans or Aztecs retreating with their treasures from insatiable Spanish Conquistadors would have arrived as refugees with all the time in the world to bury and protect their precious hoard.

Point (d), the resources and supplies issue, poses entirely different questions, however. It is a case of swings and roundabouts. The possible builders with most time at their disposal were not necessarily those who would have been likely to be well-supplied. Naval or military engineers would have been properly provided with regulation rations — Spartan but adequate. Drake's men, suffering the horrendous privations of most Elizabethan seafarers, would not have been as well-provisioned as a naval or military group in the eighteenth century.

Templars and their accompanying Master Masons on a late fourteenth-or early fifteenth-century expedition would have been less well-provisioned than Drake's men: not through any failure of Sinclair generosity, but simply because the ability to store and ship the necessities for a long journey were not there to the same degree that was developed in later Tudor times when maritime activity expanded dramatically.

Vikings and Welsh sea raiders would have been likely to travel light as far as stores and provisions were concerned. They lacked preservatives and facilities for long campaigns. What Mayan and Aztec refugees might have carried is largely speculative. Ample quantities of thoroughly dried maize carried in large earthenware containers are certainly feasible, and one alternative interpretation of the inscription on the mysterious stone is that it is a message explaining how to cut off the water by dropping large quantities of corn or millet into the beach drains. Scientifically this might well have worked. As the grain expanded, it would have blocked the drain and temporarily cut off the water. Once the grain had rotted, the water would flow again and the deadly trap would be more or less reset. So Mayan or Aztec refugees might have had not only time and ample food supplies, but an ingenious way of circumventing and re-springing the water trap.

The fifth consideration — (e) the motivation — is probably the most important of all. Human beings climb mountains, canoe over rapids and try to fathom challenging mysteries like the Oak Island Money Pit just because they are there. Given the necessary motivation, men and women can perform feats of daring courage or dogged persistence over long, hard years. What then was so important to the original miners that the deep shaft, the artificial beach, the connecting tunnels and all the back-breaking toil that went into creating them were readily acceptable? Human motivation is hard to understand. We do not always recognize our own reasons for doing or wanting things. Why does an enthusiastic philatelist mortgage his house and sell his car to acquire one more small, grubby, paper rectangle to place in the album in his safe? Why does a rock climber risk life and limb to scale a precipitous overhang when there's a grass path on the other side up which he could stroll to the summit with his dog and his grandmother on a warm summer afternoon?

There seem to be three major possibilities:

(i) Something was considered to be so uniquely valuable that only a depository as secure as the Money Pit was adequate. The motive was to preserve that immensely precious thing and to keep it safe.

(ii) Something was considered to be so sacred and holy that it must not be profaned or disturbed. The motive was to guard that holy thing, or that holy person's body, in the most effective way.

(iii) Something was considered to be so potentially dangerous (infinitely worse than plutonium or the anthrax bacillus) that it had to be made totally secure.

Every previous investigation into the Money Pit mystery has been concerned with the fundamental concept of keeping intruders out. What if all those elaborate defences, the platforms of oak logs, the putty, the fibre and the charcoal were designed to keep something in? Look at a top security prison: its prime function is to keep people in — yet a visitor from another world might be forgiven for thinking that it had been designed to keep people out.

Is it just barely feasible that the Oak Island motive was to prevent something from escaping from the depths of the pit?

Point (f), the final consideration of who was personally responsible for the whole scheme must wait for a later chapter.

All those extensive and elaborate drains and tunnels which Jotham B.McCully and his Truro excavators found in the mid-nineteenth century had to be there for a reason, a reason that was of overriding importance to the engineering genius who constructed them.

Whatever else they failed to accomplish, McCully's men found that amazing water trap and tunnel system and laid their findings out clearly for every subsequent investigator to puzzle over.

6

THE SECRET OF THE ANCIENT TIMBERS

Despite the expensive failures of 1849 and 1850, there was great enthusiasm to have another go at the Money Pit. Many veterans of the Truro Company wanted to try again and news of the amazing artificial beach and flood tunnels encouraged fresh investors to join them.

A new organisation, The Oak Island Association, also headquartered in Truro, was inaugurated in April 1861. Adams Tupper and Jefferson MacDonald were veterans of the 1849/50 expeditions, as was Jotham McCully. The leader, Samuel Retti, and James McNutt, the secretary, treasurer and official log keeper, were new to Oak Island work. John Smith, the last of the three original explorers, had conveyed his Oak Island land to his sons, Thomas and Joseph, before he died. The boys sold it to Henry Stevens and he in turn sold it to Anthony Graves — who consequently became the major landowner on Oak Island. He made an advantageous deal with Retti's organisation which entitled him to a third of any treasure they salvaged.

The Oak Island Association began its work with two clear objectives in mind. Based on the discoveries and disappointments of 1849 and 1850, they were determined to block off the flood tunnel from the artificial beach at Smith's Cove and then pump out the Money Pit. They were convinced that a sufficiently large work force would be able to accomplish both tasks with comparative ease and simplicity.

George Mitchell was the Association's foreman of works, and with the support of over sixty labourers and half as many horses he soon had the Money Pit cleared out and re-cribbed with timber well down below the eighty-foot level. At this juncture the heavy clay soil, which had slid into the shaft during the decade since work had last ceased (when the Truro team had failed) seemed to be blocking the flood tunnel quite effectively. Mitchell gave orders to stop digging at that point and shift operations to the flood tunnel.

Down through the bone dry, brick hard clay they cut a shaft nearly thirty feet east of the Money Pit. At 120 feet they gave up: their interceptor shaft had missed the elusive flood tunnel. This is not altogether surprising when due consideration is given to the problems which the original miners would have encountered. Various natural obstacles, principally boulders, must have lain between Smith's Cove and the lower levels of the Money Pit. Did the original builders follow the line of least resistance, going round a boulder here, following a seam of looser sand there? Intercepting the flood tunnel would have been like trying to locate a hidden corkscrew in total darkness using a long, thin knitting needle.

Frustrated and anxious to get results, Mitchell decided to repeat the now almost monotonously familiar technique which had invariably failed in the past: he cut yet another parallel shaft just a few feet west of the Money Pit. A horizontal tunnel a yard wide and four-feet high was then driven from the base of this new shaft towards the Money Pit. Inevitably, water burst through and flooded this lateral tunnel as well as the vertical shaft. Mitchell's men retreated rapidly as it poured in.

For three days, horses and men tried unsuccessfully to bail it out, but with no success at all. Worse still, water was now rising in the Money Pit as well. Almost unbelievably, Mitchell now turned his attention to the 120-foot shaft again. This was the one he had first dug in the hope of intercepting the elusive flood tunnel. Once more his men began tunnelling sideways into the Money Pit and — sure enough — the water burst through again.

The only thing Mitchell could think of now was more bailing, so he rigged an arrangement of seventy-gallon casks over all three flooded shafts and allocated his full work force of horses and men to the job. They worked non-stop in shifts for almost three days and this time there were visible results: the water was at last getting significantly lower. They seemed to be on the verge of success when soft clay soil plugged the tunnel between the Money Pit and the 120-foot shaft. Mitchell sent two men down to clear it out so that the vital bailing work could continue as before. These two men were actually nine or ten feet into the blocked tunnel when they heard a crash above them that sounded like an earthquake, or a bomb going off. The mud surged towards them like toothpaste from a tube which has been dropped on the bathroom floor and inadvertently trodden on by a Sumo wrestler. They were very fortunate to get out alive.

The horrendous destruction continued like something from a violent nightmare. Thousands of feet of timber — the cribbing protecting the interior walls of the Money Pit — was shaken down into the maelstrom below and disappeared. The water boiled and foamed like a gigantic witch's cauldron. One eye witness said it looked volcanic. The lower levels of the Money Pit were now a cataclysmic ruin: the mysterious treasure chamber and its precious contents had fallen into a chaotic abyss.

Fragments of very ancient timber were retrieved by the escaping workmen. One of these "black with age" could not possibly have been part of the new cribbing which had just collapsed. Other fragments of much earlier work showed tool marks and bore holes which would have confirmed the exploratory drillings made by the Truro team in 1849 and 1850.

It would appear that the treasure chamber had been resting on some sort of thick supporting beams, or a platform, and that the work of 1803 and 1849/50 had weakened these when the explorers attempted to reach the treasure from below. The constant flooding, bailing and pumping would have washed away significant quantities of the clay in which the thick supports had once been embedded. The final straw had been the Mitchell shafts and tunnels of 1861. The stubborn old supports finally gave way and the whole structure collapsed into the unknown depths below the Money Pit.

Faced with this major set-back, the Oak Island Association fought on determinedly. They raised more funds and acquired a large cast-iron pump and steam engine in Halifax. Tragically, the boiler burst, killing one man and seriously injuring several others. The Oak Island curse had claimed the first of the seven victims whom the legend said must die before the Money Pit would surrender its tenaciously guarded secret.

In 1862 Mitchell and his men were busy digging a pumping shaft close to the Money Pit. Their plan this time was to get below the 100-foot mark and drain the water from the Money Pit into their new pumping shaft. Then, with the Money Pit effectively drained, they would again cut across horizontally and extricate the treasure from under the collapsed cribbing and other wreckage.

This time, despite the recent fatal accident caused by the exploding boiler, they were putting all their faith in a new steam pump. Their purposely dug pumping shaft went down to the 107-foot level and their pumping went comparatively well to begin with. They had got the Money Pit drained and cleared of wreckage down to at least 100 feet when the insidious old enemy reappeared. The intruding water soon exceeded the capacity of their pump. The mysterious unknown engineering genius of so long ago had once again proved that he was more than a match for the latest nineteenth-century steam technology.

Not really knowing what to do for the best and caught unenviably between the Association's shareholders and the deep blue sea, Mitchell went back to Smith's Cove in a forlorn attempt to cut off the flood tunnel somewhere near the artificial beach. Just a few yards inland, they dug with increasing desperation: at fifty feet they thought that once again they had missed the elusive tunnel.

Mitchell tried another approach. If he couldn't find the beach end, he'd find the tunnel end instead. Operations were resumed from the lowest point in the Money Pit which the pumps could keep dry for them. This time Mitchell decided to strike out horizontally. He evidently believed in the grapeshot technique: fire off enough pellets in enough directions and you'll hit your target eventually. Mitchell's problem was that he had too many directions and too many levels for the grapeshot at his disposal.

Having tried several horizontal tunnels branching out from below the 100-foot level, Mitchell decided that they were too deep to intercept the flood tunnel. His diggers tried again nearer the surface, and then once more higher still. None of these attempts reached the flood tunnel. These repeated failures drove the Mitchell team back to the beach. Time and money were both running short. There were not enough resources left to build yet another coffer dam.

An interesting interpolation at this point is to consider briefly the significance of the series of coffer dams which various treasure hunters have erected unsuccessfully over the course of nearly two centuries. None lasted. None withstood the Atlantic tides. Yet the "Unknown Genius" who built the Money Pit, the artificial beach and the flood tunnels in the first place must have constructed a perfectly effective and durable coffer dam in order to do so. Even allowing that the original work was done so long ago that the tidal levels were far lower, the coffer dam phenomenon points to an original builder with a very high degree of engineering skill, one which was significantly ahead of anything yet brought out to challenge it.

Failing a dam, Mitchell's men uncovered nearly fifty feet of box drains close to the shore and wedged clay into them. It did not even withstand the first tide, but it did find its way into the Money Pit. With clay in the beach drains, the water in the shaft became very muddy looking and discoloured. If there had been the slightest residual doubt in Mitchell's mind about the connecting tunnel, this discolouration was final, incontrovertible proof of the tunnel's existence.

Intercepting had failed; drain blocking had failed; pumping and bailing had failed. What next? Like a weary sentry patrolling back and forth along a besieged castle wall, Mitchell left the beach and dug yet another superfluous shaft south-east of the Money Pit and about thirty yards away. From its base he cut another futile horizontal tunnel to try to intercept the flood tunnel linking the Money Pit to Smith's Cove. Once more, the flood tunnel played tauntingly hard to get. When that attempt failed, Mitchell's men drove another horizontal tunnel towards the Money Pit itself. They hit it marginally above the water level which the pump was now holding at approximately 110 feet.

The expedition's carpenters cribbed the pit a few feet lower for extra security and then the diggers began horizontal explorations in all directions. There was neither sight nor sign of the missing boxes, or casks, of treasure which the pod auger had located in 1849, but in 1864 these laborious probings finally encountered the flood tunnel.

Sam Fraser, who had had a supervisory role in the work during the Association's 1864 activities, wrote a graphic account of this discovery in a letter to his friend A.S. Lowden some thirty years after the event. He recalled that the flood tunnel had entered the Money Pit at the 110 foot level and that when the diggers had cut into the intersection the force of the water had hurled around boulders twice the size of a human head. So much water had come in so fast that it had driven the diggers out until the pumps had mastered it again nine or ten hours later. Sam recalled showing the tunnel to a colleague named Hill who was an engineer. Fraser also recorded that they had explored the area close to the flood tunnel junction together for any trace of the treasure indicated by the 1849 drillings but had found absolutely nothing.

At that point the Oak Island Association ran out of money and ceased functioning.

7

THE ELDORADO
ADVENTURE

Discounting the short-lived and abortive attempt of the Oak Island Contract Company, which failed to get off the ground in March 1865, the next venture was the Oak Island Eldorado Company, founded in May 1866. One prominent organiser was A.O. Creighton who ran a book bindery in Halifax. He arranged for the mysterious slab of inscribed porphyry (found by the Onslow team in 1803) to be brought from the fire surround in what had once been John Smith's home on Oak Island and displayed in the book bindery window to attract investors.

There is a strong possibility that some ancient, genuine inscription in an obscure Middle Eastern Demotic, or some other ancient alphabet, was modified or overlaid at this time to provide the simplistic letter cypher in surprisingly modern English which can readily be decoded by a competent cryptographer to read: "FORTY FEET BELOW TWO MILLION POUNDS ARE BURIED." That would have been likely to tempt a few new investors.

Taught by the failures of earlier expeditions, the Eldorado team, more widely referred to as the Halifax Company, planned to concentrate on cutting off the flood water from Smith's Cove once and for all. Their efforts, said their prospectus, were to be directed primarily to constructing a really effective coffer dam — nearly 400 feet long and twelve feet high — all around the artificial beach and drainage tunnels at Smith's Cove. The dam was built as specified and the water duly cleared from inside it. Work was about to start on emptying the Money Pit when an Atlantic storm and an unexpectedly high tide devastated the Eldorado dam. Once again, the Old Builders had demonstrated that their nineteenth-century challengers could not match them.

With their dam destroyed, the Halifax Eldorado team began working on viable alternatives. Remembering what the pod auger had revealed in former drillings, they began exploring the lower levels with a more sophisticated encased drill. They set up a working platform above the water level and started probing. The 110-foot level yielded samples of spruce. This they thought was encouraging. The earliest findings had suggested that the treasure boxes rested on a stout spruce platform. Was that what they had now rediscovered? Encouraged by the spruce, they drilled deeper.

Just short of the 130-foot level they found charcoal, coconut fibre and wooden fragments. Four or five feet further down they found more coconut fibre together with oak, spruce and poplar. They continued their extensive drilling programme in various directions and at ever-increasing depths. They found fine sand in some places and soft clay in others. James McNutt, who was keeping a careful log of what the drill retrieved, recorded strata of blue mud, clay and gravel. Layers of water were encountered at 140 feet and again at 150 feet. Nothing else of any significance was found. The primary question is: what did those drillings mean?

The first consideration is the location. From the earliest Onslow adventures, in fact, from the earliest adventure of all in 1795, there had been a remarkable continuity. Like an old-established, nineteenth-century, traditional family business, the Money Pit explorers had passed down information from one working group to another. Two of the original finders had still been available to help and advise

Jotham McCully's team in 1849/50. McCully had been there to ensure continuity of information in the 1861 operations and later. The Eldorado/Halifax team had strong links with the Association workers who had been forced to give up in 1864 when their finances ran out. The question must inevitably be asked: "Were the Eldorado drillers working in the right shaft?"

Continuity replies with a strong affirmative. Admittedly, the eastern end of Oak Island had become a mass of water-logged shafts, tunnels and bore holes by 1866, but there can be little serious doubt that the Halifax group were drilling down into that same shaft which had once held boxes on a thick platform in 1849, those same boxes which had fallen into mysterious depths when their supports collapsed in 1861.

Was that crash merely the result of the constant under-mining flow of flood water, and the repeated weakening effect of the many fruitless attempts to drive tunnels under the treasure? Or was there more to it than that? Had the Unknown Genius at the back of the whole Oak Island system done more to protect the mysterious treasure than guard it with an artificial beach and a flood tunnel? Suppose the Unknown Genius, like some Grand Master of the chess board, had made yet more contingency plans in the improb-able event of the flood tunnels being overcome. What might those additional contingency plans have been? Assuming that an intruder had overcome the flood tunnels, how could that intruder he stopped?

Some ancient tombs and mausoleums, cunningly designed to keep out grave robbers, were provided with trap doors which would open unexpectedly to plunge intruders on to sharp spikes, impale them on protruding hooks, or simply allow them to plummet down to a stone floor sixty feet below. Did those who knew about such tech-nologies build the Oak Island Money Pit? What if, in the event of a flood tunnel failure, the whole platform on which the treasure (or the sarcophagi) rested could be triggered to collapse into the shafts?

Assuming this to be correct, it presupposes that the Unknown Genius knew a great deal about what lay below the platform on which the boxes were lying. How could such knowledge have been made available? Either that original builder had dug the Money Pit far deeper than any of the nineteenth-century explorers had guessed, or like them, he or she, had explored the lower depths with a pod auger, or sampling drill.

To speculate in a less orthodox way, what if that Unknown Genius had had access to unconventional means of ascertaining what lay below Oak Island? Although highly controversial in some circles, dowsing has many supporters. Canon J.N.T. Boston, M.A., Vicar of Dereham in Norfolk, England, for many years, was an accomplished dowser, whose uncannily accurate work the authors have witnessed for themselves. Terry Edward Ross of Pennsylvania currently enjoys a well-deserved international reputation in this field, and has expressed fascinating views about the Oak Island mystery which are covered in detail later in this volume. Terry has suggested that the group behind the Money Pit's defences carried out the work a great deal further back in time than is generally thought possible, and that they came from a culture very different from those of Canada, Western Europe or North America. If that suggestion is true, or even partially true — and Terry has remarkable gifts — then dowsing (or something akin to it) could have been an integral part of that mysterious old culture.

If we put ourselves in the place of the Unknown Genius who constructed those vital Oak Island defences and then imagine that he, or she, had the means to know what lay deeper down than the platform on which his mysterious boxes rested, then we are in a position to speculate about possible contingency plans.

Like the chess expert mentally playing several moves ahead, we imagine the flood tunnel failing. The boxes on their platform are now dangerously vulnerable: so drop them to a deeper level. The "predators" will probe lower to find them: so send them sideways, lower them at an angle out of reach of the vertical probing. This can be done easily enough if we have sufficiently accurate knowledge — via dowsing or other means — of what lies below the platform.

The Oak Island area is characterised by numerous sink-holes, caverns and cavities in the rock. Suppose that our mysterious original builder decided to arrange his spruce platform so that it would tilt its boxes down a shaft into

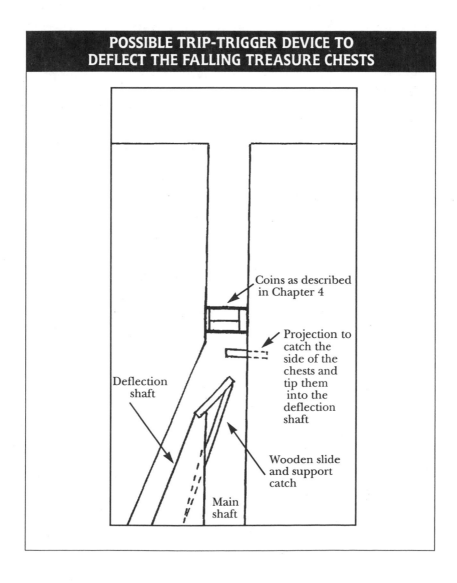

POSSIBLE TRIP-TRIGGER DEVICE TO DEFLECT THE FALLING TREASURE CHESTS

Coins as described in Chapter 4

Projection to catch the side of the chests and tip them into the deflection shaft

Deflection shaft

Wooden slide and support catch

Main shaft

just such a hole. It need not, of course, have been natural
and fortuitous: it could equally well have been modified, or
even totally artificial.

To increase the likelihood of these slide defences working,
the boxes might well have been constructed above simple
rollers, or had skids or primitive casters incorporated into
their bases. It is purely speculative, but: it does not exceed
the technology of the original builders; it does explain why
the boxes were not immediately found lower down; it also
explains why coconut fibre and wood were discovered at a
deeper level in the shaft.

If the collapsing platform, having shot its boxes off at
an angle, then tore itself loose and crashed vertically down
the Money Pit, parts of it — along with any coconut fibre
which had once been deposited on it as padding and protection for the precious boxes — would have been encountered
by vertical drilling.

As later explorations have shown, marvellous as the
Money Pit, the artificial beach and the flood tunnel from
Smith's Cove undoubtedly were, they were not apparently,
the only wonders — or even the greatest wonders — on
Oak Island. Subsequent explorations have indicated a
whole labyrinth of tunnels below the island, and at a far
greater depth than the spruce platform where the boxes
once lay. The details of those explorations and their results
will be given in chronological order in due course, but some
brief reference needs to be made to them here in an
attempt to clarify the apparently contradictory findings of
the Eldorado drillers.

In the 1849/50 pod auger work, boxes were revealed
resting on a platform between ninety and 100 feet down the
Money Pit. In the 1861/2 undermining work, something
heavy crashed down from that same level. Subsequent
attempts to locate and recover the former 100-foot platform
and its contents were fruitless. Scraps of what might once
have been the platform were located: but of the precious
boxes there was no trace.

Either they slid sideways into a previously prepared

reserve chamber, or they crashed very much farther down the shaft, or a combination of those two possibilities occurred. Were they deliberately deflected by some sort of slide mechanism so that they fell at an angle away from the original shaft? Later discoveries indicated an almost impenetrable iron barrier lower down: could that have been part of such a deflection mechanism? Did the mysterious boxes and their precious contents then descend to some vastly greater depth in the strange labyrinth far below

8

THE OAK ISLAND TREASURE COMPANY'S GREAT DISCOVERY

The Eldorado/Halifax team gave up in 1867. In terms of Oak Island history, that was a momentous year: Fred Blair was born, and he was destined to work on the mystery from 1893 until his death in 1951.

Basically, there were no serious attempts to get at the treasure between 1867 and 1893, an interregnum of over a quarter of a century, but during those quiet years there was a very interesting and significant accident on the island.

Anthony Graves had acquired what had once been John Smith's holding at the eastern end. In 1878, Graves's daughter, Sophia Sellers, was ploughing with oxen just over 100 yards from the Money Pit. Suddenly the earth opened up under the terrified animals. They crashed down into a ten foot hole, almost bringing Sophia down on top of them as the plough handles were torn from her hands. With a great deal of struggling her husband, Henry, and several more brawny Nova Scotians, finally got the oxen out of the hole. At the first convenient opportunity, Henry filled it with boulders as a safety measure. No one took any further notice of it until Fred Blair came on the scene in 1893.

He was the nephew of Isaac Blair who had worked on the island in the 1860s, and had told young Fred as much as he knew of the Money Pit mystery: yet another example of the continuity linking one generation of Oak Island researchers to the next.

Fred came originally from Amherst, Nova Scotia, and in 1893 was working as an insurance salesman. Perhaps this professional background and its concomitant necessity for checking and re-checking clients' details gave him the careful, almost scholastic attitude to the Oak Island mystery which characterised his long years of investigation.

Fred's first line of attack was to amass all the written material he could find pertaining to earlier work on the Island, and to interview all the personnel he could locate who had been involved in those earlier investigations. He spoke with such veterans as Creelman, Fraser, McCully, McDonald, McNutt and Tupper, collating and studying not only their own direct experiences but recording their recollections of information they had received from the very earliest explorers: McGinnis, Vaughan, Smith and Simeon Lynds who had led the Onslow group.

In 1893, Blair and his associates inaugurated the Oak Island Treasure Company. In their prospectus they said that a shaft thirteen feet across and 100 feet deep had been sunk on Oak Island "before the memory of any now living."This vertical shaft was connected to the sea by a tunnel several hundred feet long and at the shaft's base lay large wooden boxes of jewels and precious metals. Many previous attempts had failed, but modern technology now made it possible to succeed. The prospectus then pointed out that the treasure must be large, because so much work would never have been done to conceal and protect a small amount.

The plan was to concentrate on cutting off the water from the flood tunnel "at some point near the shore", after which it was assumed that there would be no difficulty in pumping out the Money Pit itself.

Blair's new company received such encouraging financial backing that they were able to begin work in 1894. The first thing they examined in detail was the pit which had collapsed under Sophia Sellers' oxen sixteen years before.

The first part of this work consisted of removing the boulders which her husband had placed there to prevent further accidents. Once the boulders were out, Blair's team had their first real opportunity to examine the cavity — now dubbed the "Cave-in Pit."

It soon became evident that whatever the shaft's purpose, it was contemporary with the original work: the well defined circular sides were so hard that the picks would scarcely touch them. The internal soil, by contrast, was loosely packed and easy to remove. The crew dug down about fifty feet and then drilled an experimental bore hole for almost another twenty feet. They encountered nothing — not even water.

The following day, however, the ubiquitous Oak Island subterranean water was there with a vengeance. Where had it come from?

The sides of the Cave-in Pit were practically impenetrable. They had given every appearance of defiant impermeability during the re-excavation work. It seemed very improbable that water to tidal level could have forced its way in through the small bore hole in the floor of the workings: yet there was the water, filling the Cave-in Pit and rising and falling rhythmically with the tide.

Blair's team decided that the water had gotten there via one of the many flooded drainage shafts in the area — the legacy of every failed attempt from 1803 onwards. Not really expecting to achieve anything significant, they, nevertheless, tried to bail the Cave-in Pit.

Their efforts had no perceptible effect on the level of the water. Trying to reason their way through the assortment of riddles posed by the behaviour of the Cave-in Pit, Blair's associates calculated that if it had been built directly over the flood tunnel from Smith's Cove, its collapse under Sophie's oxen and plough in 1878 ought to have affected the flow of water to the Money Pit. That hadn't happened; so Blair and his colleagues concluded that the mysterious original builders of the Oak Island system had deliberately sited the Cave-in Pit a little to the side of their flood tunnel and not directly above it. Yet, wondered Blair, why had they built it at all? What purpose could it have served? Where did it fit into their intricate overall design?

One idea which seemed reasonable at first was that it was a ventilation shaft. The popular, received knowledge about getting air into tunnels of that length (approximately 500 feet) in those days included cutting at least one vertical ventilation shaft over the tunnel. A better method, however, had already been used by miners since the mid-eighteenth century or earlier. This was an ingenious technique called a water bellows.

It worked like this. A large, sturdy tree near the mouth of the mine, or tunnel, would be hollowed out to form a rough cylinder. A wide funnel would be constructed above this so that water could be fed into it vigorously from a cascade above, trapping large quantities of fresh air as it fell into the hollow tree. Pipes from the base of the tree conducted this air and water mixture into the farthest reaches of the mine or tunnel. James Brindley gave a detailed account of this method of ventilation for subterranean workings in St. James Chronicle, dated 30/9/1763, and actually used it during the construction of one tunnel a mile long at Worsley, Manchester, England, in 1765.

Brindley's remarkable life is worth a brief glance in connection with the Money Pit mystery. Born at Thornsett near Buxton, Derbyshire, England, in 1716, he became a millwright. Buxton was at one time a famous health spa at the heart of the Derbyshire Peak District with its famous limestone crags, potholes, caves and labyrinthine underground passageways. The limestone below Oak Island has many similar features.

In 1752, Brindley designed and installed an ingenious engine to drain flooded coal workings at Clifton in Lancashire. In 1759 he worked for the Duke of Bridgwater as an adviser on canal construction. He also designed miles of underground workings for coal mines. Perhaps the most unusual thing about Brindley was his apparent ability to work without writing down any calculations or making design drawings or plans. He died on September 30, 1772, at Turnhurst in Staffordshire at the age of fifty-six.

From all the evidence he, or she, has left at Oak Island, the Unknown Genius who built the amazing structure there was of an even higher calibre than the great James Brindley. Whatever else it may, or may not, have been, the Cave-in Pit was not a simple ventilation shaft: the most convincing argument against the air hole theory must be that the Cave-in Pit did not actually connect with the original flood tunnel.

Blair's team now decided that cutting off the flood water, although still an excellent idea in theory, was not going to be the straight forward task they had originally hoped. They dug yet another useless shaft about ten yards east of the Money Pit and three yards north of where they hoped the flood tunnel might have been. The Halifax group, twenty-five years before them, had already turned the eastern end of Oak Island into a Gordian Knot of shafts, tunnels and flooded subterranean waterways. Barely forty-feet down, Blair's diggers struck one of these old Halifax workings and water promptly poured in. They left that shaft unfinished and decided to do what so many previous teams had tried already with such conspicuous lack of success: they would attempt to re-excavate the Money Pit itself.

Unfortunately for Blair's Oak Island Treasure Company, it was no longer an easy matter to decide which of the numerous filled-in shafts amidst the scarred, overgrown earth at the eastern end of the island was the original Money Pit. Blair had made many careful notes, and he still had several of the old treasure hunters to consult. As far as they knew they were working in the same shaft which McGinnis, Vaughan and Smith had dug into so enthusiastically 100 years before them. Right shaft or wrong shaft, they had not quite reached its sixty-foot level when — predictably — the flood water broke through and put an end to their work there for the time being.

Blair's backers in the Oak Island Treasure Company were partly from Boston and partly from Nova Scotia. So far the Company had got off to a very disappointing start and a quarrel now arose between the Nova Scotians and the Bostonians. The Nova Scotians won and reorganised the management team: Blair became treasurer; Perley Putnam and Bill Chappell had significant roles; and Captain John Welling was appointed site manager on Oak Island.

Under this new team the Company met with markedly more success. Work continued throughout 1896 and on into the opening weeks of 1897. The steam pumps of the 1890s were much more effective than those which had been available to earlier expeditions. By working in two interconnected shafts simultaneously, Blair's team were able to get the water level down very close to the 100-foot mark. Then tragedy struck: the supposed Oak Island 'curse' destroyed a second life.

Maynard Kaiser, a workman who lived near the local Gold River, was being hauled up the shaft on March 26, 1897, when the rope on which he was ascending slid off its pulley. There was apparently insufficient safety lip on the pulley mechanism to prevent the accident, and according to some accounts it was also overloaded: Kaiser crashed to his death 100 feet below.

The effect on the other workers was paralytic. No one was prepared to go down the shaft after the accident. There was dark talk of some mysterious and vindictive supernatural 'guardian' of the elusive Oak Island treasure. It took Blair and the other managers a full week to persuade their men to resume work.

They reached a depth of 110 feet within a month of Kaiser's death and then hit one of the lateral connecting tunnels which the Eldorado Halifax group had dug in frustrated desperation a quarter of a century earlier. Blair's men reported that the water flowing into their shaft and causing so much work for the pumps appeared to be coming from this old Eldorado/Halifax connecting tunnel. Sickening doubts began to trouble Blair, Putnam, Welling and Chappell: were they in the original Money Pit after all?

The diggers went through this old Halifax Eldorado tunnel and found another one intersecting it. They followed that one and came to a wide, dark shaft, stretching up into mysterious darkness. They looked at one another aghast in the dim light from their helmet lamps: they had only now entered the base of the real Money Pit. All their previous effort had been wasted re-excavating the wrong shaft.

Blair inspected the new shaft into which his men had just broken. Water was bubbling up fiercely from its base. All their previous work — and the tragic death of Maynard Kaiser — had taken place in an old, parallel shaft for which Adam Tupper had been responsible in 1850. According to Blair's carefully garnered records, this Tupper shaft had been driven down to approximately 110 feet and had been situated three or four yards northwest of the original Money Pit. Working on the assumption that it was this 1850 Tupper shaft on which so much time and labour had been wasted, Blair's team compensated for their earlier error by restarting their work three yards to the southeast. A few hours' digging made it clear that they were now undoubtedly in the original Money Pit. Their efforts here were rewarded by the discovery of a strange tunnel at a depth of approximately 110 feet. It boasted of no crib-work and was about a metre wide by a metre and a half high. Water was coming from it at a speed the pumps could not contend with: the diggers had to withdraw.

Blair's group convened a special management meeting to try to plan their next move. They eventually decided to try using dynamite to try to solve the problem of the pestilential flood tunnel once and for all. Having worked out a fairly accurate estimate of where it left Smith's Cove on its way to the Money Pit, Blair's men drilled a line of five holes across what they thought was its path and placed explosives in each. The third, central hole, hit the jackpot. This one went right into the elusive flood tunnel and rapidly filled with salt water up to sea level. They placed an enormous dynamite charge in it: well in excess of 150 pounds! Any tunnel which survived that would survive until

Judgement Day! When the dynamite exploded, the water in the Money Pit and the Cave-in Pit foamed and bubbled insanely. Oil from the dynamite was observed on the water's surface at both sites. At least, they had connected, but had they destroyed the tunnel completely and cut off the water?

One thing which puzzled the explorers considerably was the depth at which the elusive flood tunnel had been cut. Their huge dynamite charge had been detonated at a depth of approximately eighty feet, yet they were still very close to the artificial beach at Smith's Cove. It seemed to Blair and his associates that some sort of subterranean reservoir, or catchment chamber, had been built into the flooding system so that water collected on the artificial beach would drop into a vertical cylinder, or cistern.

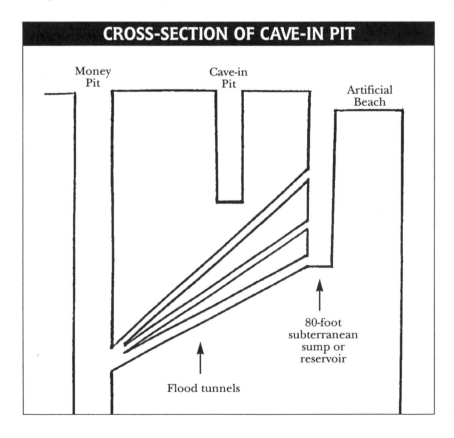

CROSS-SECTION OF CAVE-IN PIT

Money Pit

Cave-in Pit

Artificial Beach

80-foot subterranean sump or reservoir

Flood tunnels

There were difficulties and apparent contradictions, however, as far as this theory was concerned. Sea water had caused problems for previous expeditions at much shallower levels than eighty feet. Did the catchment reservoir have other outlets at higher levels? Was there, for example, one tunnel at forty feet and another at fifty as well as the major connection at eighty?

The Unknown Genius seems to have been a very devious and convoluted thinker. His flood tunnels varied not only in their horizontal turns and branches but may have had additional vertical variants as well. Such a combination would be almost impossible to eliminate in its entirety: which was exactly what the Unknown Genius seems to have wanted.

If there was only one flood tunnel, and if it was already eighty feet deep when it was less than fifty feet from the beach, how could it have admitted water to the other two shallower shafts at depths of just over thirty feet and barely seventy feet? The only reasonable explanation seems to be a plethora of flood tunnels connected both laterally and horizontally to the main tunnel as shown in the diagram.

The next course of action was to encase a two-and-a-half inch drill inside a three-inch pipe and make exploratory borings into the earth below the flood water now filling the Money Pit. As far as Blair and his associates could guess, the catastrophic 1861 collapse of whatever supports had been fixed close to the 100-foot level had allowed the treasure to fall into unknown depths. It seemed reasonable to them to assume that if they could establish cast iron evidence of its whereabouts by means of core samples, then further investment would be readily forthcoming.

The proposed drillings were duly carried out, and very curious new evidence was discovered. The drillers encountered wood at just below 120 feet. Five feet farther down there was more. At this same level, the pipe encasing their drill struck an iron obstruction and stopped.

Blair's men decided to try something smaller; they put a one and a half inch drill down without any casing.

This got past the iron and ploughed on through clay to just below 150 feet. At that depth it encountered what was either softish natural stone or man-made cement. Samples were later sent to analytical chemists who said that it had the same composition as cement, which is not quite the same thing as saying unequivocally that it actually was manufactured cement. Nevertheless, their comments were very significant: if they did not absolutely confirm that it was man made, neither did they dismiss it as a natural phenomenon. It was the famous old Scottish verdict of *not proven*.

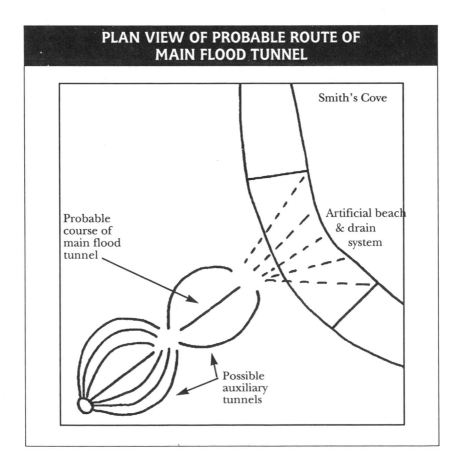

PLAN VIEW OF PROBABLE ROUTE OF MAIN FLOOD TUNNEL

Smith's Cove

Probable course of main flood tunnel

Artificial beach & drain system

Possible auxiliary tunnels

The drill went down another couple of feet and struck wood below the 'cement'. Blair's men withdrew the drill and put an auger down instead. The auger went through five inches of oak. Then it dropped a couple of inches and encountered something mysterious. None of the drillers was prepared at that stage to hazard a guess as to what it might be.

Further work gave the impression that the auger was struggling to get past bars of soft, loose metal. A sworn statement made by William Chappell, who was present at the time, maintained that whenever the drill was lifted, ready to be dropped again in order to penetrate deeper, this tantalising loose material immediately slid back into the hole. Because this made the standard drop-and-lift technique impossible, the rods had to be twisted and turned instead, while a constant downward pressure was maintained. This laborious method took the men nearly six hours to drill from the top of the loose metal to its base.

The treasure hunters deduced that they had encountered ingots of gold or silver with coins below them, and that those coins in turn were resting on another layer of ingots.

Their next plan, not surprisingly, was to try to get a pipe down where the one-and-a-half-inch drill had penetrated, and then to attempt to secure samples of whatever the drill had encountered. Either chance circumstances were against them, or the Unknown Genius had long ago anticipated this eventuality. The encircling pipe was deflected by the ancient but impenetrable iron obstruction, and went off somewhere at a tangent. It never reached the mysterious chests with their enigmatic loose metal contents. The drillers withdrew the pipe and tried the one-and-a-half-inch drill again inside the three-inch pipe. Predictably and frustratingly, it followed the diversionary hole cut by the first, deflected pipe. Blair's team never drilled into the chests again. It was like being allowed to savour the fragrance of delicious tropical fruit ripening on a distant island which you could not reach because there was no boat: so near and yet so far!

Like Gipsy Rose Lee, the Guardian of the Money Pit allowed provocative hints and glimpses — but nothing more tangible!

At about 150 feet down they encountered wood on one side of the drill and the cement-like material below it. This 'cement' continued down for seven or eight feet. It seemed to be the side, or wall, of the chamber which the one-and-a-half-inch drill had entered previously. They were now drilling through the inside edge of the wall where the boxes rested against it. At 170 feet the drill struck iron. Hours of work and careful bit tempering and sharpening penetrated this iron by less than half an inch. Magnetic testing of the recovered material produced scrapings of iron which the drill had chipped from the stubborn obstruction 170 feet below.

Careful consideration must be given to what these reported drillings could indicate. Boake Roberts, a reputable and respected industrial chemical company, analyzed samples of the so-called 'cement' and said, rather tentatively that in their opinion it was more likely than not to be man made. The most interesting and exciting possibility is that Blair's team located a treasure vault, or repository, nearly 170 feet down. Was this the same vault which had once been supported by the platform that had collapsed years before? Is it reasonable to imagine that it sank — either suddenly or gradually — while at the same time remaining intact and preserving its vital contents? If the original treasure (or sarcophagi) from the ninety-eight-foot level had been smashed and dispersed by the collapse, or diverted, or moved a long distance sideways by the flood water and the counter-productive pumping, then was this a second treasure vault which they had located at the 170-foot level?

Suppose that a mere two boxes containing a few thousand gold and silver pieces and some trinkets of jewellery had been left as a decoy at the ninety-eight-foot level to deceive an intruder into believing that that was all the treasure there was? What if the ninety-eight-foot pseudo-treasure was just one more in the long line of subterranean defences created by the Unknown Genius?

The story of Aladdin and the tale of the Magic Tinderbox both provide' interesting precedents for concealing something of immeasurable worth alongside an ordinary treasure of gold and silver.

On one of the drillings a small ball of what at first looked like wood fibre came up. Perley Putnam kept it very carefully in his personal possession until it was publicly examined by Dr A.E. Porter, who came from Amherst. The doctor subjected the tiny ball to minute examination including the use of a microscope. The ball was slowly unrolled and gently smoothed out flat. It turned out to be a scrap of parchment bearing the letters "V I" or something very similar. Dr Porter swore an affidavit to that effect on September 6, 1897. On the assumption that Putnam was an honest and honourable man — although it must be noted in passing that his Money Pit investments lost him $20,000 and practically ruined him; and that Dr Porter and the witnesses were equally honest and honourable — the evidence of the lettered parchment fragment is one of the most significant clues so far discovered.

If it can be taken at face value — and the weight of evidence is for its genuineness rather than otherwise — then a number of conclusions may be drawn:

(a)   that several strange and interesting things (other than treasure) are hidden deep below Oak Island;

(b)   that they include a mysterious old parchment document, or a number of such documents;

(c)   that whatever ancient written material is down there should provide clues to the identity of the mysterious Unknown Engineer who constructed the system;

(d)   that the parchments may also explain the real reason for the Money Pit's existence, and reveal what it was constructed to guard in the first place;

(e)   that the real treasure may comprise some arcane secret written on the parchments themselves;

(f)   that the parchments may be priceless, long lost orig-
         inals, worth infinitely more than conventional trea-
         sures of gold or silver.

There are scholarly and reputable historians who firmly
believe that Bacon was the real author of the works attributed to Christopher Marlowe and William Shakespeare.
Suppose that they are right, and suppose that to prove his
literary claims to posterity Bacon had arranged for his original manuscripts to be preserved in the New World. It
remains an undeniable possibility.

Excited by what the parchment might mean, and more
convinced than ever that an unimaginable fortune lay
below them, Blair's team attacked the island again. Having
failed to conquer the sea and the flood tunnels which conveyed it to the Money Pit, they fell back on the old, discred-
ited idea of digging more shafts and getting under the treasure. They tried this again and again, frequently running
into one of the tunnels made by the Halifax Eldorado
Company, or other earlier explorers. Every attempt failed:
shaft after shaft flooded.

Workmen's wages were in arrears. The machine hire
company wanted its back rent. The Oak Island Treasure
Company was tottering. Blair bought the other shareholders out, and there at the close of the nineteenth century the
greatest treasure hunt on earth came to another temporary
halt.

9

INTO THE TWENTIETH CENTURY

By December of 1900, Fred Blair had very astutely gained complete control of the Oak Island Treasure Company. A fifty year battle with the Money Pit lay ahead of him. For the time being, however, with insufficient resources to launch another large scale onslaught on the treasure's defences, Fred contented himself with keeping up his $100 annual lease with Sophia Sellers and his Nova Scotian treasure trove licence with the Government. His long-term future strategy was to find enthusiastic adventurers with ample financial backing who would take over the Oak Island action and divide the spoils with him when the treasure was eventually recovered.

Throughout the long years until his death in 1951, Fred never doubted that something of immense value lay below the island. Through two world wars, the Great Depression and the rush of technology from horses and buggies to nuclear bombs and computers, Fred Blair was totally dedicated to solving the mystery of the Oak Island Money Pit.

The first of his many partners did not turn out well. Captain Harry Bowdoin was a flamboyant adventurer with a flair for publicity and a background in engineering. His energy and confidence were boundless: his financial resources were not. He founded "The Old Gold Salvage and Wrecking Company" in April 1909. It had an authorised capital of $250,000 but sold barely $5,000 worth to shareholders.

Bowdoin was widely publicised in an article in the New York Herald of March 18, 1909, as a Master Mariner and Pilot. He was said to have wide engineering skills covering machinery, mining and marine work. His alleged experience included government contracts for harbours and bridges. He was also reported to be licensed as a diver. Bowdoin was brashly confident that he could " ... solve in a jiffy the difficulties Captain Kidd had made to guard his treasure ..." Bowdoin claimed that he could clear up in a fortnight the problems which all the previous treasure hunters had failed to solve over the past hundred years. It would be little more than a casual vacation for him.

There is a particularly relevant line from I Kings 20: 11, "Let not him that girdeth on his harness boast himself as he that putteth it off."

The Bowdoin offices at 44 Broadway, New York, were prestigious. So were the company's front runners: Bowdoin himself was President; Fred Blair had the Vice-Presidency; the Company Secretary was an accountant named G.D. Mosher; a New York lawyer, L.H. Andrews, was their treasurer and the same Captain Welling who had lost $4,000 during his previous entanglement with the Money Pit served on the Board of Directors. Among the $5,000 worth of shares, a few had been sold to a singularly able young lawyer named Franklin D. Roosevelt, who was then working for Carter, Ledyard and Milburn of New York.

As a child, F.D.R. had spent many summer vacations on Campobello, an island between Maine and New Brunswick. Already a competent sailor by the time he was six years old, F.D.R. met and talked to many seafarers in the area about the Oak Island mystery. When he was only sixteen, the young Roosevelt sailed with a friend to Grand Manan Island in search of Captain Kidd's treasure, which legend said lay buried there. Their expedition is strangely reminiscent of the adventure which the youthful Smith, Vaughan and McGinnis had on their first visit to Oak Island in 1795.

Small wonder, then, that F.D.R. was interested in supporting Bowdoin's treasure hunting syndicate in 1909. It was an interest that never died. Even as President, with the New Deal and World War II to occupy his attention, Roosevelt was always glad to receive reports about the latest events on Oak Island.

In his wide-ranging and abundantly confident prospectus, Bowdoin outlined his plan to locate the treasure by drilling and then to cut off the flood tunnels by driving interlocking steel sheets into them. Once he'd located the treasure and cut off the water, he intended to excavate with a bucket dredger to get the precious metal to the surface. In addition, he had a contingency plan: if all else failed he would use "Bowdoin's Air Lock Caisson." This, he proudly proclaimed, would enable the workmen inside it to go down through mud or water, to work sideways as well as downwards, and to send up any interesting or valuable finds via the caisson's air lock.

On August 27, 1909, the ebullient Captain Bowdoin and his entourage set up "Camp Kidd" on Oak Island. If all had gone as he predicted, they were scheduled to have been sailing home with their share of the treasure on or before September 11th.

The abject account of their failure makes dismally familiar reading: they couldn't find the Smith's Cove end of the flood tunnel; they made the customary unsuccessful assault on the Money Pit itself; they couldn't afford the big 1,000-gallon-a-minute pump on which so much depended; they drilled almost thirty holes but failed to touch any of the deeply buried, displaced treasure. Predictably, their woefully inadequate $5,000 soon ran out.

Before giving up on November 4th, Bowdoin had also used a diver and dynamite without success. He and Blair then had a sharp disagreement: Bowdoin wanted to come back and try again, but Blair wouldn't agree to that unless, and until, Bowdoin could satisfy him beyond any reasonable doubt that the essential financial backing was available. The dashing Captain couldn't and didn't: but he threatened

Blair that unless his search contract was renewed a report would be issued that would discourage any future investment. Blair, commendably, replied as the Duke of Wellington had once replied to a blackmailer: "Publish and be damned!"

On August 19, 1911, Bowdoin's sour grapes duly displayed their verdant acidity in the public vineyard of *Colliers* magazine. His vituperative article was entitled "Solving the Mystery of Oak Island," It formed a curiously contradictory epilogue to his company prospectus of 1909. " ... there is not, and never was, a buried treasure on Oak Island ..." Fortunately, Bowdoin's peevish and ill-founded literary outburst did little to discourage those prospective treasure hunters who had already looked objectively at the long array of evidence and decided for themselves that the balance was clearly in favour of something immensely valuable on the island.

Fred had set himself three basic criteria which future treasure hunting partners had to meet: they must have a sensible, logical, practical approach to the problem; they must have at least one competent, qualified and experienced engineer on their site team; and they must have adequate funding available. Previous attempts had almost invariably foundered on the twin reefs of inadequate engineering skills and insufficient money.

Many people approached Blair after Bowdoin's 1909 debacle and his subsequent invective in *Colliers* in 1911. Some had the hallmarks of charlatans anxious to turn Oak Island investment into another South Sea Bubble: Blair shunned them like the bubonic plague. Others arrived with honest hearts, sensible theories and empty wallets: they were politely declined. Fred finally placed an advertisement in the *Boston Journal of Commerce* on December 7th, 1922.

It was headed "Buried Treasure" and was worded with refreshing honesty and lucidity. Setting the minimum investment level at $50,000 as the price of a 50% interest in what Blair frankly called a "speculative venture," it offered "a sporting opportunity" to make millions set against the very real risk of losing most of the stake. Blair made it very plain that this was a venture suitable only for someone who could comfortably afford to lose $50,000.

A fascinating editorial in the *Journal* supported Blair's advertisement and suggested that Sir Henry Morgan (1635–1688), the famous Welsh pirate and one-time lieutenant governor of Jamaica, had hidden the treasure he stole during his famous Panama raid somewhere on Oak Island.

It took Blair almost twenty years of careful sifting and frequent disappointment before he found the partners he needed, and significantly, they had already been associated with his earlier activities between 1895 and 1900.

In 1931 William Chappell, who had once been one of the managers of Blair's Oak Island Treasure Company, was a part-owner of Chappells Ltd with premises in Sydney, Nova Scotia. Chappells was prosperous enough to allow William and three other members of the family, his son Mel, and other relatives, Claude and Renerick or Renwick, to launch an Oak Island project in conjunction with Blair. William himself had been involved in the drilling work over thirty years before, when the parchment fragment had been recovered.

Mel was a qualified engineer and a member of the Canadian Institute. He talked through the problem with professional colleagues and the consensus was that a well-cribbed shaft would be the best approach. An electric pump capable of shifting between 400 and 500 gallons a minute was brought to hold down the water level. The Chappells's first problem was the exact location of the Money Pit. Bowdoin had butchered most of the older structures, including the cribbing and drilling platforms. With the passing of twenty years and more most of the earlier re-excavations had collapsed. The Chappells had William's memory and Fred's memory as their main guides: and, unfortunately, the two veterans disagreed by a crucial six feet. They compromised by digging their shaft twelve feet by fourteen, in the hope that at least part of it would overlap the original Money Pit of 1795.

This generously proportioned Chappell shaft went down over 160 feet and the team then drilled exploratory holes another ten or twenty feet deeper. In all that distance they found no cement chamber, no wooden boxes, no iron obstructions: nothing, in fact, which had been drilled through in 1897. They did, however, dredge up an ancient anchor fluke which probably dated from the fourteenth or fifteenth century, and an Acadian axe of a slightly later pattern. Between the 120-and-160 foot levels they also encountered tools and timbers, apparently relics from earlier expeditions: but these were as much as twenty feet lower than the recorded working depths of the nineteenth and early-twentieth-century shafts. Quite how they had sunk down that extra distance remained a mystery to Blair and the Chappells.

Several possibilities might account for their failure to strike anything significant. Their shaft could have missed the vault by a few feet; even one foot would have been enough — and Blair himself thought the Chappell shaft was at least six feet away from the original Money Pit. Another strong possibility was that a combination of Bowdoin's clumsy dynamiting and the constant pumping of millions of gallons of flood water had eroded so much of the original workings that the former chamber had collapsed or been filled with waterborne debris.

The sinister and mysterious 'guardian' envisaged in the Money Pit legends was apparently working overtime during the Chappell expedition's activities in 1931. George Stevenson the foreman was almost crushed to death when a tunnel caved in. One man lost an eye, others suffered broken ribs. The weather was foul. Storms knocked out the electrical supply to the pump. Work on the drainage system and flood tunnel from Smith's Cove was also an expensive failure. Dynamite was tried once more — and once more it failed. Further samples of coconut fibre were unearthed, but no significant progress was made towards cutting off the flood water. Then Mel Chappell made one very impor-

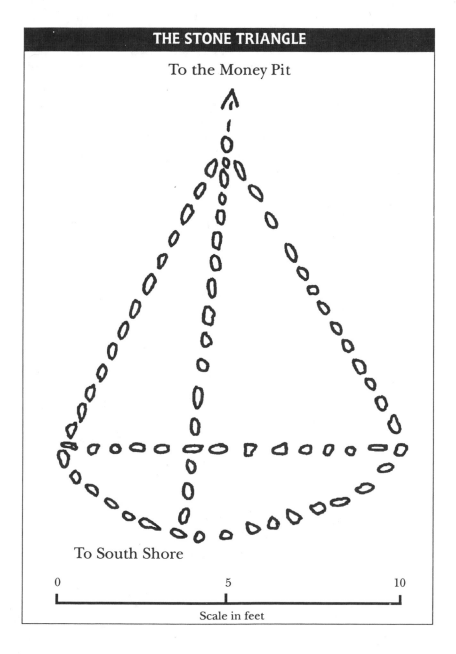

THE STONE TRIANGLE

To the Money Pit

To South Shore

0   5   10

Scale in feet

tant rediscovery: in 1897 Captain Welling had found a curious stone triangle in the shape of a sextant. One marker line of that triangle pointed unerringly towards the Money Pit. Welling had shown it to Blair during the 1897 workings, but for some reason it had not been regarded as important at the time, and had subsequently been forgotten. One theory current among the Chappell team was that the stone triangle had been constructed by a previous treasure hunting expedition for some purpose of their own — perhaps to mark the exact position of the Money Pit. Later researchers have given rather more thought to the stone triangle and its possible significance. Tragically, like other important clues such as the inscribed porphyry block, the stone triangle was obliterated: victim of the high-powered stop-at-nothing approach of a later researcher armed with a multi-ton earth mover!

By the end of October $40,000 and six months' hard work had produced almost nothing for the Chappell team. Then a new problem arose for them. Sophia Graves, Anthony's daughter, had married Henry Sellers. They had owned and farmed the eastern lots on Oak Island — including the notorious Cave-in Pit into which Sophia's ploughing team had fallen in the spring of 1878. Henry had already been dead for some years before the Chappell team started work in 1931. Sophia died while the work was in progress. When the legal formalities cleared there were no fewer than a dozen heirs who all adamantly refused to renew Fred Blair's $100 a year lease on the island, on which the Chappell deal depended. The problem with Sophia's heirs did not affect Fred's licence from the government, but it seriously limited access to the site.

Curiously enough, the Sellers heirs did grant permission to Miss Mary B. Stewart who led a group of investors. In 1932 they hired John Talbot, an engineer from New York, to do the actual site work. His team drilled for two months, reaching depths of 150 feet but finding nothing.

In 1933 Thomas M. Nixon from Victoria in British Columbia founded the Canadian Oak Island Treasure

Company. Nixon's theories were based on legends of lost Inca treasure, deposited under Oak Island by refugees from Peru who had fled from the Conquistadors. Nixon was also a convinced supporter of the decoy theory: a few minor pieces in the boxes at high level and a vast quantity in the depths. Had the necessary finances been available, Nixon had intended to sink interlocking steel piling in a great circle around the Money Pit. The public failed to take up more than a handful of the $225,000 worth of shares issued, so Nixon had to content himself with drilling a few experimental holes. He located: seams of pink sand which were probably the result of the red dye experiments from the previous century; fragments of old oak below 100 feet; pieces of pottery below 120 feet; something which he described as an oak and cement bulkhead; and a cavity of more than thirty feet before encountering more ancient oak and solid matter at approximately 180 feet. All very intriguing, but equally inconclusive.

In November of 1934 Nixon gave up and left the island, leaving the way clear for the next contender: Gilbert D. Hedden.

Hedden was a much more formidable challenger for the Unknown Genius and his cunning defences. Having first become interested in Oak Island from reading an article in the *New York Times* (May 8, 1928), Hedden had spent seven years thinking how best to approach the engineering challenge which the Money Pit presented. In 1935, Hedden was a vigorous and highly intelligent thirty-eight year old with more than enough spare money for the Oak Island adventure, plus good engineering qualifications and years of management experience in the Hedden Iron Construction Company based in Hillside, New Jersey. He had also had good business experience in insurance and car dealing and had been elected Mayor of Chatham in 1934. Gilbert Hedden had the money, the engineering background and the proven managerial experience.

He paid an extortionate price for the Sellers' land: $5,000. If the possibility of recovering the treasure is ignored, the rentable value of that land was less than $20 a year as pasture. That would have meant a return of 0.4 per cent or less than a tenth of the totally safe interest available from U.S. Treasury Bonds in the 1930s: a period when the safety of their investments was paramount to most people. The possibility of locating treasure had inflated the price of the land ten fold.

Gilbert Hedden had one mental attitude in common with the Emperor Napoleon: he believed in hiring experts and then listening to good advice. In the days of Napoleon's early successes this worked exceptionally well: it was only when he forsook this policy that political and military dis-

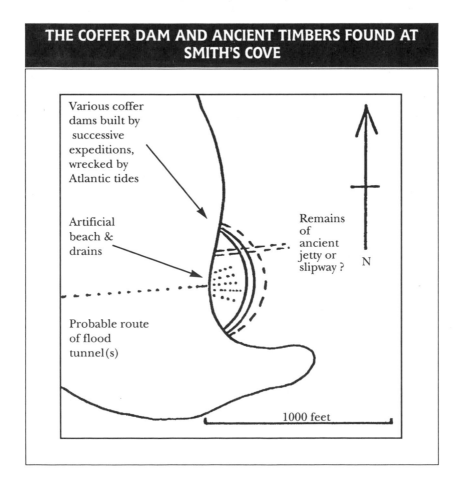

THE COFFER DAM AND ANCIENT TIMBERS FOUND AT SMITH'S COVE

Various coffer dams built by successive expeditions, wrecked by Atlantic tides

Artificial beach & drains

Remains of ancient jetty or slipway ?

N

Probable route of flood tunnel(s)

1000 feet

asters overtook him. Hedden went to Pennsylvania and hired Sprague and Henwood to get rid of the water and re-open the Money Pit.

Hedden had chosen well. Sprague and Henwood were a very good professional firm and their work proceeded with crisp efficiency and accuracy led by Frederick Krupp and Sylvester Carroll. They had a 1,000-gallon-a-minute pump which seemed more than a match for the flood water. Starting in the former Chappell shaft, they went down 170 feet: deeper than any of their predecessors had gone. They then took a new shaft (the Hedden shaft) down to approximately 125 feet. This was even wider in cross section than the big Chappell shaft to give plenty of room for the horizontal, exploratory drillings which it was proposed to make at two-foot intervals. The Sprague and Henwood approach seemed to offer the best chance to date of recovering whatever the Unknown Genius had interred below Oak Island. Between ninety and 100 feet, the diggers hit clay or putty of the kind brought up in the previous century. They also drilled through many pieces of oak at about 150 feet: some were barely an inch thick, others had a girth of as much as six or seven feet. There was every indication that some of these were the remains of the chests and their supporting platform, which had collapsed in 1861 when Mitchell's men had attempted to get underneath them. Pieces of oak at this depth were a strong indication that the Sprague and Henwood drillers were very close to making a major find: perhaps even the treasure itself. Another intriguing discovery which encouraged Hedden and his team consisted of what appeared to be the remains of a very ancient ramp, jetty or slipway (or perhaps even an ancient coffer dam) running from the artificial beach beyond the line of the coffer dams and out into the Atlantic. This jetty, or whatever it was, comprised massive old timbers with notches and bearing Roman numerals. Forty years later, Dan Blankenship and the Triton team were to discover just how extensive these old timber workings were.

Hedden had every intention of resuming work as soon

as the winter ended but it was not to be. He had already spent at least $50,000 before the end of 1937; then financial disaster struck in the shape of huge tax demands connected with his profits from the sale of a steel business he had owned in 1931. Years of expensive litigation left Hedden perilously close to bankruptcy, but he maintained a rather wistful watch over the island until 1950.

Hedden's strange encounter with Harold Wilkins and the notorious "map of Skeleton Island," attributed to Captain Kidd, form part of chapter 11, which looks into the various theories linking pirates and privateers with the Oak Island Mystery.

With Hedden prevented from further on-site explorations because of his financial difficulties, the way was clear for Professor Hamilton to take up the Oak Island challenge. He taught engineering at New York University in the 1930s, and was ideally qualified to search for a solution to the problems posed by the Money Pit and the flood tunnels. As Hedden still owned the land, and Blair held the Government treasure-hunting licence, the three men had to work out a deal under which Blair would receive 40 per cent (instead of the 50 per cent he had originally negotiated with Hedden), while his two partners would then be due for 30 per cent apiece.

Hamilton rehired Sprague and Henwood, who now added recent first-hand experience of Oak Island drilling to their other considerable professional recommendations.

Throughout five summers, Professor Hamilton worked carefully and systematically on solving the Oak Island mystery. Employing over a dozen men and spending an estimated $60,000 between 1938 and 1943, he continued working despite the problems caused by World War II.

He drilled out sideways from the wide Hedden shaft, but encountered nothing more revealing than pieces of old oak, which he concluded were either nineteenth century cribbing from the various tunnels, or from the disastrous collapse of 1861.

During the next few years, Hamilton explored many of

the old shafts and workings from previous expeditions and made a number of interesting discoveries: but he failed to establish anything conclusive. One of his exploratory drillings penetrated limestone bedrock over 200 feet below the surface and brought up oak chips from that depth. He also repeated the dye experiments made in 1898; he and his colleague, Amos Nauss, went out in a boat and saw their dye coming up from the sea-bed three or four hundred feet off the South Shore. At least one flood tunnel starting as far out as that must have connected with the Money Pit at a depth in excess of 150 feet.

Hamilton never returned to New York: he decided to stay in Nova Scotia where he joined Nauss in a boat-building venture in Marriot's Cove, where he died in 1969.

Over the years, Oak Island has made more money for the lawyers than for the treasure hunters. After Professor Hamilton had given up and become a boat-builder, Hedden eventually sold his land to John Whitney Lewis, a New York engineer with almost forty years' experience. Lewis thought he'd obtained the essential Government treasure licence along with the land, but Blair had renewed it for himself in 1950 to run for a further five years. The lawyers got involved when Lewis wouldn't allow Blair on his newly acquired land. However, it was legally possible in certain circumstances to obtain a Treasure Trove Act Special Licence which gave the holder permission to trespass in the course of his, or her, treasure hunting activities, provided always that no damage was done. If it was, the licence holder was legally bound to pay the landowner compensation. Lewis naturally contested this situation, but lost. Thoroughly unhappy about the whole venture by this time, he accepted Mel Chappell's offer for the land and retired from the Oak Island arena.

Early in 1951, Blair died and Chappell acquired the vital Treasure Trove Licence to go with his land purchase: the all important Plot Eighteen and the Government permit were now both in the same hands. But as with the earlier Chappell explorations, Fortune seemed to have turned her back. Just as the Middle Ages were infested by characters like Chaucer's Pardoner and various confidence tricksters pretending to have access to the Philosopher's Stone, so the twentieth century has been plagued by scam artists with mysterious 'gold-finding' machines. Ironically, some of these 'inventors' may have been sincere: in such cases they deluded themselves as well as their clients. A weird-looking machine bulging with what appeared to be scientific circuitry was brought to Oak Island in December 1950. Its inventor told Mel Chappell that there was a large deposit of gold within twenty feet of the surface. He indicated an area only fifty yards from the original Money Pit. Chappell paid to have a huge steam-powered earth mover brought over to the island. Then he paid for a vast hole to be dug in the area the 'gold-finder' had indicated. Nothing of any value came out. The machine indicated other locations: Chappell paid to have drillings carried out in those areas. Nothing of any value was encountered. The work cost him nearly $40,000, but he had learnt a lot from the experience: principally, that any future investments in treasure hunting had to be made by someone else. In return he would issue a free lease, including the use of his Government treasure hunting permit, on condition that he was to have 50 per cent of any treasure recovered.

George Greene, a burly, cigar chewing Texas oilman, did a deal with Chappell in 1955. As with so many other researchers, Greene had family connections with earlier Oak Island explorers: John W. Shields had been involved with Bowdoin's ill-fated work in 1909, and John was George Greene's uncle! Like any veteran oilman, George believed in exploratory drilling. He announced that it was his intention to drill all over the island looking for the mysterious 'concrete vault' and its precious contents. He had more than one string to his bow: if he didn't find the treasure vault, he was off to drill for oil in South America; he also believed that Hollywood might be interested in filming the Oak Island story, and that he'd stand to gain from the film rights if they did. Greene had plenty of confidence, and there was almost unlimited Texan oil money behind him. His main finds were tantalising wood fragments from various depths, and a vast cavern — so big that the 100,000 gallons of water he pumped down to try to ascertain its volume simply disappeared.

Greene's theory was that whatever was buried on the island had come originally from Spanish South American sources, and probably dated back to the sixteenth century.

The brawny Texan eventually left Oak Island to take on a new drilling contract in Louisiana, and his consortium's deal with Chappell ran out. The pressure of the Louisiana contract and some later work kept Greene away from the Money Pit. He never had the chance to return. He was murdered in British Guiana while taking part in geological work there in December of 1962. Nothing more than a tragic coincidence, perhaps: it was certainly dangerous and unstable country then — but there are those who would hint that he was yet another victim of the nebulous and sinister Oak Island 'curse.'

When the Texan oilmen's contract with Chappell expired, the Harman brothers, William and Victor, from Ontario, took over. Like the unfortunate George Greene, they believed that the treasure was Spanish in origin, and that it had been plundered from South America in the sixteenth century. Their extensive deep drilling programme produced oak fragments, coconut fibre, pieces of spruce and 'putty', or ship's caulking clay. They were convinced that they were on the right track: then their money ran out, and another curious legal stand-off arose. Chappell would not renew their lease unless they could convince him that they had enough funds to make a worthwhile attempt to recover the treasure. The Ontario Securities Commission prudently declined to allow them to set up a stock-selling public company to raise those necessary funds unless they had a minimum five year lease on the treasure site. It was a classic 'Catch 22' situation, and the Harmans were defeated by it.

The courageous and resilient Restall family were the next contenders. As a boy, co-author Lionel Fanthorpe watched a dare-devil fairground motorcyclist named Terry Ward performing death-defying stunts inside a twenty foot steel mesh sphere called the "Globe of Death." The show was visiting Great Yarmouth, in Norfolk, England at the time — the late forties or early fifties. There were several other members of Ward's stunt team, whose names are not now known. (Terry was clearly recalled because he signed autographs after the performance which Lionel watched!) It is possible that Mildred and Robert Restall were members of the team performing in Norfolk that day.

Robert and Mildred married in 1931 when she was a seventeen-year-old ballerina and he was on tour as a young stunt rider. They developed their thrilling "Globe of Death" act together and toured Europe and North America with it for over twenty years. In 1955 they visited Oak Island where Robert met the luckless George Greene, who gave him an account of the Money Pit mystery. That chance meeting changed the Restalls' lives and led to a grim multiple tragedy ten years later.

After Greene and the Harman brothers had abandoned their attempts and left the island, Robert Restall prevailed upon a group of friends to provide the necessary minimal financial support to add to his own life savings. In 1959, having signed a contract with Chappell, Robert and his eighteen-year-old son, Bobbie, moved on to the island and began.

Despite their meagre financial resources, they put in a tremendous amount of work together over the next five years, without making any major discoveries. Mildred and nine-year-old Rickey joined them on the island, where the family home consisted of two small temporary living rooms without any amenities. With characteristic courage, determination and optimism the Restalls battled on — absolutely determined to solve the Oak Island mystery and recover the treasure.

Robert had been concentrating his efforts on cutting off the flood tunnels as an essential first step, and had dug a shaft nearly thirty-feet deep between the Money Pit and

Smith's Cove. On August 17th, 1965, he had a small gasoline-engined pump rigged above this shaft, and running continuously. As a result there were only a few feet of water in the bottom. The weather that day was exceptionally hot and oppressive, which may have contributed to the impending disaster.

It is not certain what caused Robert to fall. Perhaps he had been leaning over the side looking down; perhaps he had been descending the ladder between the pump and the shallow water below. In either event, young Bobbie saw that something was seriously wrong and raced across to the shaft to help his father. Seeing him lying motionless in the water, Bobbie shouted for help and began to climb down. Within seconds he, too, had fallen and lay unconscious in the water. Robert's friend and partner, Carl Graeser, arrived next in response to Bobbie's earlier shouting.

He was closely followed by sixteen-year-old Cyril Hiltz, another loyal member of the Restall team. Carl and Cyril went straight down to help the Restalls with no thought for their own safety: both intending rescuers also collapsed unconscious into the water. Andy DeMont, also a faithful Restall supporter, scrambled down to try to help. He, too, fell from the ladder.

At that point in the tragedy, Captain Ed White, a professional New York fire-fighter who was visiting Oak Island as a tourist, came on the scene. He realised instantly that some sort of toxic gas — either methane seeping from the shaft, or carbon monoxide from the pump's engine — had overcome the men in the pit. With the help of several courageous volunteers — James Kelzer, Richard Barder, Peter Beamish and others — Captain White went down on a rope and secured the unconscious Andy DeMont. He tried desperately to help the earlier victims but was on the verge of losing consciousness himself as the other volunteers hauled him out with DeMont. Both men revived with the help of artificial respiration. Firemen from Chester later recovered the bodies of Carl, Cyril, Robert and his son.

Triton Alliance, led by David Tobias and Dan

Blankenship, who are currently conducting the Oak Island search, erected on the site a memorial notice board which pays tribute to the Restalls and their companions, and gives details of the tragedy and the courage of the would-be rescuers.

Dan Henskee with the Restalls' Memorial notice.

Dunfield's Causeway completed on October 17th, 1965. Oak Island was no longer an island.

The long, hard struggle which the dauntless Restalls had put up had been seriously handicapped by lack of funding and a consequent shortage of heavy earth-moving and drilling machinery. If they had used too little equipment, there are many Oak Island experts who would shake their heads disapprovingly and say that the next contender, Californian geologist Bob Dunfield, had used far too much!

Dunfield came from Canoga Park and had graduated from the University of California in L.A. He attacked Oak Island in the same way that Hannibal's elephants had attacked the Roman army at Zama: it was a powerfully direct, if somewhat unsubtle, approach. In an earlier age, Bob Dunfield might have made a highly successful cavalry commander, but Oak Island defeated him as decisively as Scipio had defeated Hannibal! Dunfield began by constructing the causeway which now links Oak Island to Crandall's Point on the mainland in order to get his seventy-ton crane-digger to the island: barges had been able to carry his bulldozers, but the crane was beyond the capacity of any barges or rafts available in the vicinity. As from October 17, 1965, Oak Island was no longer an island — Dunfield's Causeway was completed.

He moved the crane with its ninety-foot arm and huge digging bucket over to the Money Pit end of Oak Island, and began work. The first four yards of topsoil had already been bulldozed away from the surface of the Money Pit zone to expose the tops of numerous old shafts — including the Money Pit itself.

Dunfield hacked a massive twenty-foot-deep trench along 200 feet of the South Shore in a search for the second flood tunnel. He didn't find it, but he did encounter an old shaft over forty-feet deep that appeared to have been part of the original pre-1795 operations on the island. This curious and apparently purposeless shaft was within thirty feet of the inexplicable stone triangle. Dunfield then launched a direct attack on the Money Pit itself, turning it into what looked like the site of a World War II tank battle fought out during a severe monsoon season. He created a hole over 100 feet across and nearly half as deep again.

Just as the Chappell expedition of 1931 had been dogged by a very unusual run of bad weather and other problems, so was Bob Dunfield's work. His equipment suffered so many mechanical breakdowns that the question of sabotage was raised. Certainly his new causeway was not popular with local boatmen who now had to detour around the far end of Oak Island, and his *Blitzkrieg* methods in the Money Pit area were not welcomed by Nova Scotian historians and archaeologists.

In Dunfield's defence, it must be acknowledged that he arranged for all the excavated earth to be carefully rinsed and examined, and a great many fragments of early seventeenth-century pottery and china were found.[4]

---

[4]It would be worthwhile to submit specimens of this pottery to Edinburgh or Copenhagen Universities where the techniques of thermo-luminescent glow-curve dating of pottery have been pioneered. In essence, a fragment of the ceramic is placed inside a dark chamber and heated. Depending upon how long ago it was last fired, it will glow when a certain temperature is reached. Pottery fired in Roman times, for example, glows at lower temperatures than pottery fired in the fourteenth century, and that, in turn, glows at lower temperatures than Victorian pottery. Thermo-luminescent testing has already verified the age of some of the controversial objects found on M. Fradin's farm at Glozel, near Vichy, France, in 1924: another intriguing unsolved mystery which may well have connections with both Rennes-le-Château and Oak Island.

Dunfield then replaced most of the soil and resorted to drilling. His work confirmed Greene's discovery of the huge cavern below its limestone roof. He next turned his attentions to the Cave-in Pit, and scooped it out to a depth of over 100 feet with a diameter to match: nothing came up except a few old timbers, which he attributed to the industrious tunnelling of the Halifax/Eldorado Company in the previous century.

In the spring of 1966, Dunfield gave up and went back to California — approximately $150,000 worse off for his experience with the Money Pit. Oak Island, too, was much the poorer: the old stone triangle, which might have provided a vital clue to the mystery if only it had been studied properly, slid away into Dunfield's trench during heavy rain and was lost forever. Dunfield himself died in Encino in 1980.

Lionel Fanthorpe and Emile Fradin beside the Glozel Museum containing the mysterious artifacts which M. Fradin discovered in 1924.

Patricia Fanthorpe at the site of the Glozel discoveries.

10

TRITON ALLIANCE
TAKES OVER

Prior to his untimely death, Dunfield had made his contribution to the continuity tradition linking all the Oak
Island expeditions: he had become one of the earliest shareholders in Triton Alliance, the company currently working
to solve the Money Pit mystery.

It was Dan Blankenship, David Tobias and the earliest
of the Triton Alliance pioneers who now took over the main
line of the search, but in order to understand the current
situation fully, Frederick G. Nolan's parallel work has to be
taken into account. In 1958, he had read *The Oak Island
Mystery* by Reginald V. Harris, the Halifax lawyer who had
once acted for both Blair and Hedden. Nolan also knew
Harris and had discussed the mystery with him. In 1958,
however, the way was not clear for Fred to do any work on
the Island: the Harman brothers were still busily making
their unsuccessful attempt, and Robert Restall was next in
line.

Although Chappell was unwilling to sell the island to
Nolan, and steadfastly refused to grant him a treasure
hunting lease because he was hoping to attract some really
wealthy speculator who could recover the treasure and
share it with him, he did give Nolan permission to conduct
a thorough professional survey. It was carried out with
painstaking accuracy and proper professional skill in 1961

and 1962, and it cost Nolan a great deal of time and money to complete.

Because Chappell had steadfastly and consistently refused all of his approaches, Nolan — a man of considerable determination — tried another line of attack. As a skilled and experienced professional surveyor, he found it easy enough to check the land registry: and there he hit the jackpot! Chappell did not own the whole of Oak Island after all — he only thought he did: plot five and plots nine through fourteen inclusive were not his. They had never been transferred since 1935. Technically, at least, they still belonged to the heirs of Sophia Sellers. Nolan acted swiftly and decisively: he bought them.

Nolan's approach was predominantly concerned with looking for and recording interesting old artifacts, survey stones and boulders with holes chiselled into them. He has drawn numerous lines and patterns connecting the markers he has discovered, and some unusual and significant shapes have emerged. It is not unreasonable to assume that there may be something substantial in Nolan's theories, and his latest ideas and discoveries are described in detail in William S. Crooker's very readable and well researched *Oak Island Gold* (Halifax: Nimbus, 1993).

The great and continuing problem of this parallel work is that relationships between Triton Alliance and Nolan have never been cordial, and have frequently been downright hostile.

There was trouble initially between Nolan and Bob Dunfield over the use of the new causeway in 1965. Nolan then bought land at Crandall's Point (the mainland end of the causeway) and put up a barrier across it to prevent the causeway from being used at all. Dan Blankenship took over from Dunfield in 1968 and arranged a temporary truce, first by paying Nolan for the right to cross his land at Crandall's Point, and later by offering him shares in the Money Pit treasure in return for carrying out survey work for him and his new partner, David Tobias, on their part of the island.

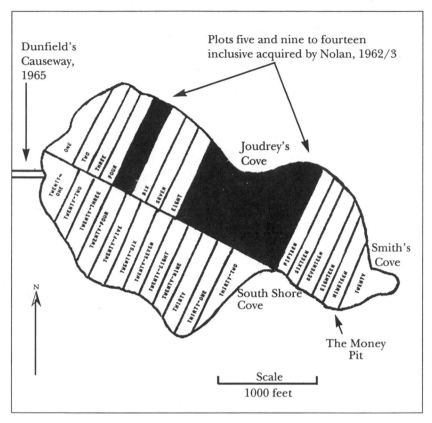

This brief truce ended in 1969 when Triton Alliance was formed. The ensuing years saw a long and unfortunate series of claims and counter-claims, court actions, mutual irritations and retaliatory hindrances between Triton Alliance and Nolan. It is ironic to think that the money both sides spent on litigation and court costs could have gone a long way towards financing further important exploration, drilling and surveying on the island. Reconciliation does not seem likely at this late stage, but all things are possible — and without doubt it would be of enormous benefit to both parties if only it could be achieved.

Oak Island explorers either get involved by hearing fascinating accounts from previous treasure hunters, as Simeon Lynds did in 1803, or by reading about the mystery somewhere. Dan Blankenship read an excellent article on the Money Pit in *Readers Digest* in January 1965, which was a condensation from *The Rotarian* magazine. That article changed his life dramatically. In 1965, Dan visited the island where he met the Restalls and Dunfield, from whom he took over the operation the following year. He knew Hedden, Professor Hamilton and Chappell, and he made the most of the vital information and long years of experience which those veterans had to offer.

The authors first met Dan and his family in 1988 while doing some early site research on Oak Island for their "Unsolved Mystery" lectures in the U.K., and spent a very informative and enjoyable time discussing the Money Pit with the Blankenships then and with Dan again in October of 1993. He is very powerful and impressive: a man of massive mental and physical strength and stamina; a man with genuine depth of character. He inspires complete and fully justifiable confidence. If anyone this century is going to recover the amazing treasure that lies somewhere in the labyrinth below Oak Island, there is no doubt that he will be the man to do it.

After teaming up with David Tobias, who had already supported the Restall investigations, Dan became the field operations director for Triton Alliance, a reliable and substantial organisation with prestigious shareholders including: Bostonian property developer Charles Brown; Gordon Coles, former attorney general of Nova Scotia; George Jennison, one-time president of the Toronto Stock Exchange; and Pentagon weapons expert Bill Parkins.

Fascinating discoveries have already been made during the systematic drilling, exploring and excavating programmes which Triton have carried out under Dan's direction on the island. In 1966, below the level which Dunfield had reached in his South Shore shaft, an old hand-wrought nail and a metal washer were unearthed. Lower still, a layer of large round stones was found. They had evidently been placed there deliberately: were they part of the old South Shore flood tunnel? In 1967 Dan found a 300-year-old pair of scissors under one of the drainage lines below the artificial beach at Smith's Cove. There was also a metal set-square which dated back at least to the eighteenth century, and a very odd-looking heart-shaped stone which gave every appearance of having been deliberately carved at some date in the remote past. In 1970, the erection of Triton's coffer dam in Smith's Cove led to the discovery of the rest of the massive timbers, the first of which Gilbert Hedden had found thirty years before.

These huge lengths of wood, which lay in a 'U' shaped formation, were two-feet thick and as much as sixty-feet long. Each bore a different Roman numeral, and each was notched at four-foot intervals. Holes bored in the notches were fitted with wooden dowels — a technique that pre-dated nineteenth-century work when iron and steel were readily available, cheap and convenient. The whole structure must have been a massive undertaking — of the size and quality which Oak Island researchers associate with the original work designed by the Unknown Genius of long ago. Expert opinion tends to the view that this huge wooden structure may have been a combination of coffer dam and slipway, or jetty and landing stage.

In 1967, dozens of exploratory drillings were made deep into the labyrinth below the island, and wood was frequently found below the bedrock at depths well in excess of 200 feet. When these drilled samples were subjected to radio-carbon dating the results showed them to range from approximately 350 to 500 years old. There is, however, a problem with radio-carbon dating of oak: everything depends upon what part of the tree is sampled.

Imagine that a 100-year-old tree is felled and used to make part of a Norman cathedral roof in 1100 AD. If the sample taken to the laboratory is drawn from the heart-wood of the tree, it will give a date nearly 100 years different from that which would be obtained from a sample close to the bark. The nearer the chosen fragment is to the bark, the more accurate the dating will be.

Historians could not really be certain from their radio-carbon dating alone whether that particular section of the Cathedral's roof had gone on in 1000 AD, 1200 AD or some date between the two. (Any year pre-dating the Norman Conquest would, of course, have to be discounted — but that decision would be based on historical knowledge other than that provided by the radio-carbon test.)[5] Among leading experts who examined the prodigious old timbers was Dr. H.B.S. Cooke who taught Geology at Dalhousie University in Halifax. Dr. Cooke's opinion was positive and unequivocal: the structure was evidently man-made and was, in all probability, a coffer dam.

In 1970, Golder and Associates of Toronto, widely recognized as leading specialists in geological engineering, conducted a definitive survey of the island for Triton Alliance. Golder's engineers gave their opinion that a complicated labyrinth — a perplexing mixture of man-made workings and natural formations — exists deep below Oak Island. The more explorations were made, the more extensive these strange underground workings were seen to be.

In this aspect, too, Oak Island sounds uncanny echoes of Rennes-le-Château. What began there as a simple enquiry into how an impoverished nineteenth-century Parish Priest suddenly became rich, has expanded over the years into one of the most challenging mysteries of all time. There are weird patterns on the ground covering distances of several miles among ancient landmarks, tombs and cromlechs. Murders remain unsolved. The complex geometry of Nicholas Poussin's paintings and a church full of pictures and statues conceal esoteric clues to an ancient and terrible secret. What did the eccentric and secretive Priest, Bérenger Saunière, find there over a hundred years ago? And where did he conceal it again shortly before his death in 1917?

Another of Triton's significant discoveries took place in

---

[5]Radio-carbon dating was developed at the University of Chicago in the late 1940s. The basis of the technique comprises a comparison between the relative activities of ^{14}C (the radioactive form of carbon) in contemporary living tissue and in the sample being dated. The logarithm of this ratio then has to be multiplied by the rate of decay of ^{14}C. The half-life of ^{14}C is normally reckoned to be 5568 years ±0.54 per cent an uncertainty equivalent to ±30 years out of the 5568.

1970 in what is now known as Borehole 10-X. The Bowmaster Drilling Company took it down to 230 feet under Dan Blankenship's instructions, and then blew compressed air down the hole to bring up anything of interest in the material loosened by the drill. Thin metal scrapings which rapidly oxidised on exposure to the air, lengths of old wire and fragments of chain came up from between the 160 and 170 foot levels.

So many interesting and inexplicable finds were being made in 10-X that Triton wisely decided to enlarge it sufficiently to admit an underwater television camera. Watching the tape which that camera recorded is an eerie and perplexing experience: like so many other important Oak Island clues, it tantalises and intrigues the researcher, but falls short of providing final and absolute proof of exactly what is down there or how it got there. The tape shows passages with well-defined corners and rectangular apertures which seem more likely to have been the work of man than the work of nature. They look as though they might well be cribbed with straight timber frames. The natural anhydrite bedrock does not characteristically form tunnels of this type. The swirling water which the camera had to penetrate was flecked with small moving specks — like a light fall of snow — and this detritus material had settled over many of the objects which lay in the mysterious depths. There was a slim curved shape which could have been an old mariner's cutlass. There were also several large cuboids, their rectangular edges softened by layers of settled material from the floating 'snow storm.' Were they boulders, ancient storage boxes, treasure chests or coffins?

In August 1971, Triton worker Dan Henskee and Parker Kennedy, a drilling expert from Halifax, were with Dan Blankenship when the camera revealed what appeared to be a severed human hand floating in the murky waters deep inside Borehole 10-X. Later photographs revealed what looked like a waterlogged but remarkably well-preserved human corpse. A sealed compartment filled with salt water and excluding the air would be capable of preserving human remains for centuries.

Phil Irwin of Atlantic Divers Ltd., with headquarters in Brooklyn, Nova Scotia, went down well below the 180-foot mark, where the one-quarter inch steel lining of 10-X ended. The force of the subterranean current at that depth almost tore the helmet from his head, and the masses of suspended particles brought visibility down to zero. Muddy water in Smith's Cove showed where the fierce current was originating. It looked as if 10-X had penetrated at least one of the Unknown Genius's ancient flood tunnels, and diverted the flow downwards into the labyrinth far below.

Blankenship's team bulldozed tons of clay over the entrance in Smith's Cove, and another dive was made. The terrifying pressure of the racing water had stopped, but visibility was still close to zero. The divers dared not stray far from the foot of 10-X; their lights revealed almost nothing; feeling around on the floor of the mysterious cavern revealed only small stones.

After that, Dan himself made several dives, but again the problem of hopeless visibility and the danger of moving more than a few feet from the base of the shaft were too great — it was impossible to locate the salt-preserved body, the chests, or any of the other strange objects which the camera had revealed.

The pumping was also causing rapid erosion of the anhydrite, so that the original cavity was becoming bell-shaped, and too dangerous for a diver to enter.

The inventive Bill Parkin — with as much flair as the legendary 'Q' in Ian Fleming's 'James Bond' novels — made several major contributions to the available technology. One piece of equipment which he provided made it possible to measure salinity in the flood tunnels, which revealed that not all the water was coming from the Atlantic. A liberal supply of fresh water from somewhere was moving around under Oak Island.

In November 1976, Dan was nearly 150 feet down in 10-X cutting an observation window into the shaft's steel lining while his son, David, operated the winch above. There was

Lionel and Patricia Fanthorpe with Dan Blankenship and a section of the crushed steel tubing which collapsed in November 1976 while Dan was still 150 feet down the shaft.

a strange, ominous rumble, and the sound of something massive hitting the steel above Dan's head.

Sensing his danger, Dan used his telephone link to signal to David to haul him up immediately. With the Restall tragedy of 1965 uppermost in his mind, David ran the winch at full speed. Dan could hear more threatening noises above him. They were louder and closer: the steel tubing was about to collapse inwards upon itself — and him — at any second! Sixty feet higher than when he had first heard the warning thuds against the steel cylinder, Dan looked down. The shaft just below him was now crushed in like a rusty old car body shell caught in a junk metal dealer's fifty ton press He had escaped with barely seconds to spare.

And there — more or less — is where the physical exploration still stands today. Like every other attempt to solve the mystery of the Money Pit, money is the main problem. Triton Alliance (despite their massive financial resources) do not yet have the estimated $10 million plus which expert engineering consultants believe would be necessary to dry out the labyrinth below Oak Island and find the answer that has eluded searchers for two centuries. Meanwhile, Blankenship and his men go on drilling. Nolan goes on surveying and drawing lines between his marker stones.

There is, however, a third and very important line of attack — historical investigation, research and theoretical speculation. Resolving the problem of what is hidden in the labyrinth, and who put it there, by deduction, may be the single most important step towards recovering it.

The boys who started this great treasure hunt in 1795 were convinced that pirates, or privateers, were responsible. How much support does history give their theory?

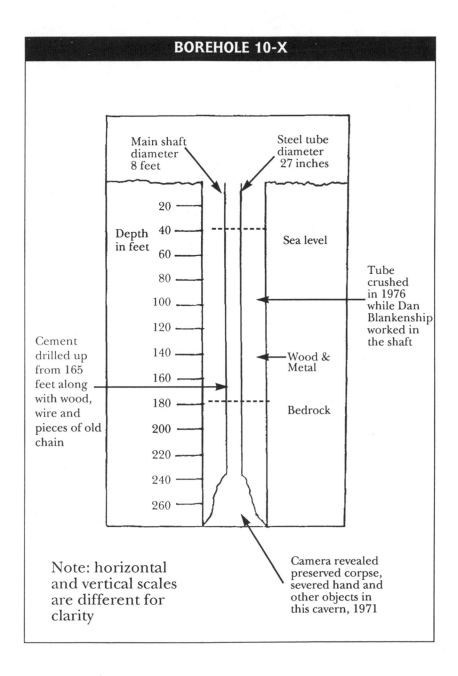

BOREHOLE 10-X

Main shaft
diameter
8 feet

Steel tube
diameter
27 inches

Depth
in feet

20
40
60
80
100
120
140
160
180
200
220
240
260

Sea level

Tube
crushed
in 1976
while Dan
Blankenship
worked in
the shaft

Wood &
Metal

Bedrock

Cement
drilled up
from 165
feet along
with wood,
wire and
pieces of old
chain

Camera revealed
preserved corpse,
severed hand and
other objects in
this cavern, 1971

Note: horizontal
and vertical scales
are different for
clarity

Dan Blankenship and Lionel Fanthorpe beside the machinery at the head of Borehole 10 -X.

View down Borehole 10-X.

11

PIRATES AND PRIVATEERS

Although Robert Louis Stevenson's world famous *Treasure Island* did not appear until 1881, its realistic portrayal of pirate atmosphere is timeless. Flint, Black Dog, Blind Pew and Long John Silver were not destined to reach the bookshops until nearly a century after Smith, Vaughan and McGinnis reached Oak Island and made their pioneering discovery — but lurid tales of Henry Morgan, William Kidd, Woodes Rogers, Edward Teach and other infamous pirates were widely known and frequently retold in eighteenth century Nova Scotia.

A long tradition has associated the Oak Island Money Pit with William Kidd, but how likely is it to have any basis in historical fact? Popular accounts suggest that Kidd was born in 1645, the son of the Reverend John Kidd, the Calvinist Minister of Greenock in Scotland, but there is little or no reliable evidence for these assertions. Paul Lorrain, Prison Chaplain at Newgate when Kidd was hanged in 1701, says that the pirate was then in his mid-fifties, which gives some validity to the approximate birth year.

Almost nothing is known of Kidd's early life, but from 1689 to 1691 there are records of his successful work as a privateer captain against the French in the West Indies. Kidd married the twice-widowed Sarah Bradley Oort on May 16, 1691. She was only fifteen when she married her first husband, William Cox, who had been a wealthy New York alderman. He died when she was eighteen. Her second husband, John Oort, had been a prosperous shipmaster and merchant. He had been dead for just over a week when she and Kidd took out their marriage licence! William and Sarah owned what must now rate as some of the most valuable property in the world: 86–90 Pearl Street, 52–56 Water Street, 56 Wall Street and other premises.[6]

Sarah's connection by marriage with the Oort family is a strange coincidence, and may turn out to have more significance than appears on the surface. Ort, Orth and Oort (Latin *ursus*, French *ours*) are variations of a word meaning 'the bear.' The semi-legendary Arthur of Britain, Celtic King and/or Romano-British Warlord of the West, was closely associated with the bear in folklore and mythology. The Rennes-le-Château mystery has a strong link to the Habsburgs, particularly to Johann, a descendant of the Tuscany branch, who denounced his title, took the surname of Orth, became a sea captain and allegedly went down with his ship, the *Saint Margaret,* in 1890, somewhere off Cape Horn.

This *Saint Margaret* tragedy was, of course, a full two centuries after Kidd's involvement with John Oort's widow, but that New York Oort family may well have had Habsburg connections, and John's mercantile marine activities would certainly have involved trade with Europe and Asia. Might some important Oort information that Kidd heard from his new wife have provided the spur that sent him on what was ostensibly a privateering voyage to the Indian Ocean?

In the days before the Suez Canal was cut, Indian and Asian goods, silk, spices, jewels and tea, had to be sailed laboriously around the Cape of Good Hope. This brought the precious cargoes perilously close to Madagascar and the small islands nearby — notorious pirate strongholds. The East India Company — wealthy and influential at the

---

[6] See pamphlet entitled *New York's Land-holding Sea Rover* (New York: Lotus Press, New York Title and Guarantee Co., 1901.)

Court of William and Mary during the last decade of the seventeenth century — put massive pressure on the British Government to provide warships to deal with the pirates who were destroying their trade.

New York and the American North Atlantic ports (forbidden officially to undertake manufacturing or to trade other than via British ports and British ships under the terms of the Navigation Acts) were not at all averse to taking part in the illicit Madagascar trade. A privateering commission could be bought very cheaply in New York at that time, and everyone benefited from the goods the privateers brought back.

One version of Kidd's enlistment, as commander of the privateer that the East India Company had demanded, was that he was more or less coerced into the job through fear of being thought disloyal, or unenthusiastic. It was rumoured that Kidd's greatest ambition was to captain a Royal Navy man-o'-war, and that failure to accept the East India privateering commission would permanently bar him from achieving his own quarter-deck to strut on!

Whatever his true motives — and it seems more probable that Kidd had some special private and personal task in the Indian Ocean — or beyond — rather than that he was merely allowing the British Government to pressurise him — he set out as captain of the *Adventure Galley*. She was a 287-tonner carrying only thirty-four guns — hardly a match for the formidable pirate vessels she was meant to pursue. He signed seventy rather dubious crewmen to start with, and almost immediately ran into his first problem. While his vessel was anchored impudently beside HMS *Duchess of Queensborough,* as though claiming the prestige and privilege of another Royal Navy vessel, Kidd was visited by the press gang who 'recruited' the best twenty of his crew. He complained bitterly to Admiral Lord Russell that he now had scarcely enough hands left to sail the *Adventure Galley* without attempting to take on the extra burden of fighting well-manned, well-armed and well-equipped corsairs. Eventually, he got twenty men back —

but they were very inferior to the men that he had lost to the *Duchess*.

Having captured an almost worthless French fishing boat and used most of what it fetched to buy provisions in New York, Kidd took his time about sailing for the Indian Ocean, a delay which irritated his powerful British backers. Eventually, with an even less reliable crew than he had started with, Kidd sailed for Madagascar. Was that delay really caused by Kidd's need to consult further with Sarah and her brother who sailed with him about some vital information they had obtained from the late John Oort?

He sullied his reputation again by insulting British Naval Commodore Warren whose squadron he encountered off the Cape of Good Hope. Then fifty of Kidd's crew died of disease in Mehila in the Comoros. In July of 1697 he laid wait for the Mocha merchant fleet, but ran into the fearless, efficient and well armed Captain Edward Barlow, Master of the *Sceptre,* who was guarding the convoy with more guns than Kidd had. In the face of Barlow's spirited action Kidd and the *Adventure Galley* retreated ignominiously. His subsequent kidnapping of an English Captain and his Portuguese Mate from a Moorish vessel did little to enhance Kidd's rapidly deteriorating reputation. He quarrelled with Moore, one his gunners, and then gave him a fatal blow with an iron-bound wooden bucket. One of the charges which cost Kidd his life in 1701 was Moore's murder.

Some time later he captured the only worthwhile prize he ever took, the 500-ton *Quedah Merchant:* it was Kidd's fatal misfortune that she had an English Captain named Wright and was the lawful property of Armenian merchants against whom Kidd had no warrant.

Kidd and his captive 'fleet' reached Madagascar on April 1, 1698, and sailed into the notorious pirate harbour on St Mary's Island. Here he encountered his old enemy Robert Culliford, now a successful pirate captain. Kidd ordered his untrustworthy men to attack Culliford's frigate, the *Mocha,* but they disobeyed him derisively, deserted to join Culliford, and ransacked Kidd's ships. He was lucky to escape with his life, and a proportion of his non-too-plentiful spoils.

There is now a period of some uncertainty in Kidd's life during which he might just have had time to reach Oak Island and bury his treasure — if he had still had anything worthwhile left to hide, which is highly doubtful. Abandoning the conspicuous and slow-moving *Quedah Merchant* under guard in the Higuey River in Hispaniola, Kidd acquired the anonymous-looking sloop *Antonio* and reached Long Island in her. Sarah and their two daughters joined him, but, from there onwards, Kidd's life was all downhill: betrayal, desertion, imprisonment in horrendous conditions, sickness, condemnation, death by hanging and finally rotting on a gibbet for years at Tilbury Point.

Three years later, while the pathetic remnants of his tarred body still hung there, Sarah remarried and lived comfortably for another forty-odd years in New Jersey.

The chance that Kidd had anything of value to bury at Oak Island, or that he had ever possessed the men, the money or the engineering skill to construct even one-fiftieth part of the incredible workings there, must produce odds of hundreds to one against — and yet a tiny lingering doubt remains. There is the odd business of Sarah's second husband, John Oort. Could he have been one of the 'bear clan' associated with the ancient and powerful House of Habsburg? As such, did he know anything about the secret Arcadian treasure, part of which may have been concealed at Rennes-le-Château? Did Oort, perhaps, leave papers or a map in a strong-box which the beautiful but illiterate Sarah asked Kidd, her third husband, to read and explain to her? Was there something in those papers which tempted Kidd to find an excuse — even a dangerous and unwelcome privateering excuse — to get to the Indian Ocean (or beyond it to the South China Sea) to try to retrieve something of immense value connected with that mysterious Arcadian treasure? The chances are very slight indeed, yet they do not recede to zero: it is only possible to say that Kidd's involvement in Oak Island is very unlikely.

In this strange Money Pit investigation, however, nothing is entirely impossible, and there is still the disturbingly coincidental 'evidence' of the Wilkins' Map to be considered.

What purported to be a map of the location of Kidd's treasure cache turned up in a book by Harold T. Wilkins published in London in 1935: *Captain Kidd and his Skeleton Island*. This composite, which Wilkins admitted that he had largely drawn from memory fertilised by imagination, was based on several so-called Kidd charts which had been 'discovered' by Hubert Palmer, an English antiques dealer who specialized in pirate relics. Palmer had allowed Wilkins to see the 'original' maps at a distance, but not to copy any of the bearings or other directions which they contained. Nevertheless, when Wilkins' book appeared there were cryptic directions on the composite sketch map he had drawn!

Gilbert Hedden's lawyer, R.V. Harris, came across Wilkins's book and was intrigued by the superficial similari-

ARTIST'S IMPRESSION OF COMPOSITE MAPS, POSSIBLY PERTAINING TO KIDD'S "SKELETON ISLAND"

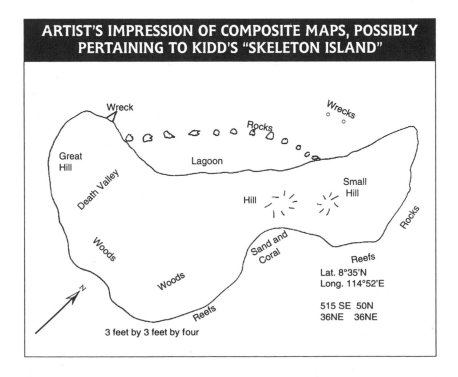

Drilled boulder observed and photographed by the Fanthorpe team in 1988.

ty of the Wilkins' version of Skeleton Island to Oak Island. He drew these similarities to Hedden's attention. Book in hand, Hedden tried to interpret and follow the directions. They led him to a drilled boulder north of the Money Pit.

When he excitedly told Blair about it, Fred remembered seeing a similar drilled boulder forty years previously. The two of them relocated it and began pacing out distances: as a result they called in Charles Roper, the Provincial Land Surveyor with his assistant, George Bates. Roper's and Bates's work led to the stone triangle, and a site line from the triangle's pointer indicated the Money Pit! It all seemed far too accurate to be a coincidence. Hedden flew to England to interview Wilkins.

Here he was grimly disappointed. Wilkins insisted that his map, which was in any case partly imaginative and partly a composite, referred to an island in the China Sea and had nothing whatever to do with Nova Scotia or the North Atlantic. Hedden pressed him about the directions shown below it; Wilkins said he might have seen them on one or more of the thousands of maps and charts he had studied in the course of writing his various books about piracy and buried treasure. When Hedden finally succeeded in convincing Wilkins that markers (the drilled boulders) had actually been found very close to the places indicated on the semi-imaginary map, Wilkins was amazed. According to Hedden's later account, Wilkins then began trying to convince himself that he was a reincarnation of Captain Kidd and had somehow produced the map and its accompanying instructions from some deep sub-conscious memory!

There is one more incongruous data-fly struggling around in this speculative ointment: French was widely spoken by the Acadians (Arcadians?) in the area in the early settlement days, and *chene* is French for "oak". Was the China Sea that was marked on what purported to be the treasure map a slight misrendering of the French *Chene*, or Oak, Sea — meaning the sea around Oak Island: in other words, Mahone Bay?

Putting it all together, a wildly improbable — but just barely possible — Kidd scenario begins to emerge. A map, chart, or other curious document relating to the Arcadian treasure is discovered by William and Sarah among the late John Oort's papers. The main feature of this information is a reference to the China Sea. William and Sarah discuss the safest and most legitimate way to get there. In pursuit of an excuse to visit the pirate infested South China Sea in an adequately armed vessel, Kidd goes to London on board his own sloop the *Antegoa*, where he meets the wily Colonel Livingstone and the potentially untrustworthy Bellamont, the newly appointed Governor of New York. Secretly backed by four influential and unscrupulous British Government peers (who insisted on anonymity) Kidd sets off on his ill-fated voyage in the *Adventure Galley*. His reluctance to tackle real pirates, or well armed enemy vessels, now becomes much more understandable: he is trying to cross the Indian Ocean in one piece and then negotiate the Straits of Malacca to reach the South China Sea.

His reluctance to assuage his mutinous crew's thirst for piracy also becomes more understandable: he does not wish to risk bringing a British war fleet down on the *Adventure Galley* because his piratical activities have been reported by survivors. Out of favour with his sponsors and with his crew, the hapless Kidd fails miserably to reach the South China Seas because his men desert him and flock over to join his old enemy, the pirate Culliford. The irony of Kidd's tragedy is that he had only to sail a few miles up the much less hazardous Atlantic coast to find Oak Island in its Chene Sea. The question then arises of what happened to the Oort map, or, perhaps, a copy of it which Kidd made and initialled? Did William manage to pass it to Sarah before the end, and did it eventually get from one of Sarah's descendants to the mysterious Captain Allen, who cruised enigmatically around the Oak Island area with it for two summers, but apparently found nothing?

Captain Allen — if that was his real name, which is doubtful — was a wealthy southerner who turned up in Chester, on the shore of Mahone Bay, a few years after the end of the American Civil War (1861–1865). Allen had a mysterious map (the Oort-Kidd Arcadian document?) which he consulted daily, but allowed no-one else to see. He bought a small ship from a Shad Bay fisherman named Ganter and spent day after day sailing from a location about thirty miles out on a course that should have brought him to Oak Island — but never did.

After two long summers of this fruitless search, Allen left the area and handed the quest over to a Halifax man named Pickles. More communicative by nature than Allen had been, he referred to a treasure 'so huge it was beyond imagining[7]' and an island with three stone markers and a mysterious 'well.' (Could the Money Pit by any stretch of the imagination have been described as a vast 'well'?) Did Allen and Pickles get into St Margaret's Bay rather than

[7]See the reference to the 'limitless' Cathar Treasure, *pecuniam infinitam,* which disappeared from the mountain fortress of Montségur, France, in 1244, described in *Secrets of Rennes-le-Château,* R.L. Fanthorpe and P.A. Fanthorpe, (York Beach, Maine: Samuel Weiser Inc., 1992), 44.

Mahone Bay because of magnetic variations over the years? Or were they misled by differences of nomenclature that had occurred? The old Des Barres survey referred to Mahone Bay as Mecklenburg Bay, and listed what is now St Margaret's Bay as Mahone Bay! Not surprisingly, therefore, Pickles apparently had no more success than Allen.

If William Kidd is discounted as highly unlikely, might it have been the flamboyant Welsh swashbuckler, Sir Henry Morgan (1635–88), who was responsible for the Money Pit and its ancillary defences?

There is almost as much mystery and confusion over Sir Henry Morgan's early life as over Kidd's. In his will, Morgan referred to his 'ever-honest cozen, Mr Thomas Morgan of Tredegar,' but he himself seems to have been born in Llanrhymney, in Glamorgan. He was a successful buccaneer who later became deputy governor and a justice of the peace in Jamaica, ironically sitting in judgement over many of his former corsair associates.

Unlike Kidd, Morgan was a charismatic leader against whom few chose to rebel, and even fewer dared. His most likely connection with the Oak Island Money Pit relies on his incredibly well-planned raid on Panama involving a force of nearly 2,000 buccaneers according to some accounts. In January of 1671, Morgan led his indomitable pirates and their allies through miles of swamp and jungle, although his marauders were so hungry at one point that they were reduced to eating leather. On the eighth day of their advance they were ambushed by Indian archers, but came through with enough survivors to carry out the great attack on Panama itself. The Spanish defenders greatly outnumbered Morgan's men, but were no match for them in combat. The Spanish infantry were cut to ribbons by the deadly accuracy of Morgan's musketeers; the flower of the dashing and fearless Spanish cavalry were decimated by the unerring aim of Morgan's French allies.

A Spanish ruse to stampede cattle into the backs of the attacking buccaneers misfired badly when the wily Morgan got his pirates clear in time and then encouraged the terrified animals to charge on into the remaining Spanish defenders!

After Morgan's victory, there was considerable confusion about the spoils. Some accounts averred that a number of Spaniards had managed to escape south on two galleons loaded with gold and jewels; others reported that long mule-trains packed with valuables had left for Mexico before Morgan took the city. There is considerable room for doubt. Many of the buccaneers complained bitterly that their share of the loot was far smaller than expected. Does that suggest that Morgan, supported by an inner circle of trusted veterans, had made other arrangements for at least half the Panama takings? It is a reasonable assumption.

Morgan certainly had enough cash, rank and leadership skills to have enabled him to organise an expedition on a grand enough scale to have constructed the Oak Island labyrinth. Did he have the motive, the necessary quantity of valuables to conceal and the opportunity? Perhaps he did. If the discontent among the disappointed Panama raiders had rumbled on, and the finger of suspicion had continued pointing to Sir Henry, then he would have had ample motive to construct a deep, secure treasure vault. He could well have been planning to retrieve his huge fortune in fifteen or twenty years' time, when the buccaneers' suspicions would have evaporated, but his dismissal from all his official posts in Jamaica in 1683 and his death there in 1688 brought those plans to nothing. Morgan is by no means the most likely candidate for role of Money Pit maker, but he is an undeniable contender — and a far more probable one than the hapless and ineffective Kidd. Like Lloyd George, the great statesman, and Tommy Farr, the courageous heavyweight boxer, Sir Henry Morgan, the charismatic buccaneer, was a formidable Welsh warrior — a man who normally achieved whatever he set out to do.

If personality, determination, leadership and charisma, like Morgan's, are necessary qualifications, then Drake also demands serious consideration. Born sometime between 1539 and 1544 in Tavistock, Devon, England, of sturdy yeoman farmer stock, Sir Francis Drake was undoubtedly a man of exceptional ability. His skills as a navigator were among the highest in the world — which he circumnavigated between 1577 and 1580. Before this, he had been one of the most successful corsairs who ever raided the Spanish Main, and his attack on Nombre de Dios was one of the outstanding exploits of maritime history. His plunder from the Spanish treasure ship *Cacafuego* contributed substantially to the estimated half-million pounds which he brought home to Queen Elizabeth.

Drake was also the principal architect of the destruction of the Spanish Armada in 1588. He died of dysentery on January 27, 1596, with the blazing ruins of Puerto Bello as his memorial pyre.

Could Drake have been connected with the Oak Island mystery? Certainly he had the ability, the powers of leadership and organisation, and the unquestioning loyalty of enough strong and capable men to have carried out the work there. During many periods of his hectic life, he also commanded enough wealth to justify the construction of at least part of the complex Oak Island system. But are there enough gaps in the historical records to allow him the necessary time for that enterprise? It is certainly possible. His best opportunities would have arisen between 1573 and 1575, and again between 1585 and 1587, and it could be argued that he would have had additional motives for the work: a safe base on the Nova Scotian coast for refurbishing and careening his ships, together with a safe hiding place for treasure which was less than legitimate. It would have been preferable from Elizabeth's point of view for her trusted pirate-admiral to have kept a safe (and anonymous) store for her on Oak Island than for him to sail into England too blatantly and too frequently with what was obviously stolen gold from the New World — especially during diplomatically tense periods of fragile peace in England's cold war with Spain.

The most wildly breath-taking historical hypothesis of all is that Elizabeth's very close and secretive relationship with Drake was more than platonic. There have always been persistent rumours that the immensely talented Sir Francis Bacon was, in fact, Elizabeth's child, and that the fanatically loyal Protestant Bacons (Sir Nicholas and Lady Ann) smuggled him out of the palace and pretended that he was theirs. If the rumours have any foundation in fact, and if Drake was Bacon's father as well as the mysterious architect of the Money Pit, then the Baconian connection with Oak Island becomes much more probable (see Chapter 16: Francis Bacon's Secret Cypher).

Two more intriguing questions arise in connection with the doughty Sir Francis. Referring to Drake's activities in 1573, Dr. A. J. Williamson writes: "He disappeared so effectively that to this day no-one knows where he was in the next two years, which are an absolute blank in the record."[8]

The indigenous Micmacs of Nova Scotia have intriguing, centuries-old folk memories and legends of a mysterious hero named Glooscap, who came to them in a "great stone canoe with trees on it, a canoe as big as an island." In Andrew Sinclair's excellent book, *The Sword and the Grail*, it is convincingly argued that Glooscap was Prince Henry of Orkney. It is equally possible in view of Dr. Williamson's research that Drake's mysterious missing years from 1573 until 1575 were spent helping the Micmacs, who dubbed him Glooscap in their later legends. Perhaps with their assistance in providing some of the manpower, he constructed the Money Pit and its defences while he was there. A period close to 1573 would certainly fit the radio-carbon timber dating perfectly!

---

[8] Ernle Bradford, *Drake* (London: Hodder & Stoughton, 1987), 96.

12

CELTS AND VIKINGS

The term 'Celts' is taken from the Greek *keltoi* and Latin *celtae,* which referred to the peoples inhabiting much of the Iberian peninsula and transalpine Europe from about 700 BC and possibly earlier. Around 400 BC they began vigorous emigrations into the Balkans and Italy. They were a powerful, gifted race: wild and dangerous in war, but aesthetically talented, intuitive and mystical in their art forms, their music and their literature. Great travellers, adventurers and traders, pioneering Celtic groups moved from Europe to the British Isles at an early date.

Celtic warriors sacked Rome in 390 BC and there are records of Celtic ambassadors talking with Alexander the Great in 335 BC Certainly, they were a people to be reckoned with: a people who have left many of their bold, indelible marks across the pages of history. Is it possible that the amazing Oak Island labyrinth is another such mark? Many of the oldest Celtic legends, especially the Irish *imramha,* refer to travelling and voyaging. There are tales of journeys to Iceland and Greenland, and to less well-defined destinations which may very reasonably be assumed to include America and Nova Scotia. The Celtic heroes of these legends make epic voyages to the magical lands of eternal happiness far beyond the western ocean.[9]

An interesting example is the seventh-century work,

part verse and part prose, in which Bran the son of Febal meets a mysterious woman who offers him a silver apple branch and calls him to her land of Emain (the Happy Otherworld) which lies far across the sea to the west of Wales and Ireland. Taking three companies with nine men in each — 'magical' numbers here, the square of three and the cube of three — Bran sets out. Their first landfall is the Island of Joy; their second is the Land of Women. Here the leader of the Women helps them to land by using a magical clew[10], and they stay with her people for what seems to them to be about a year. Finally overwhelmed by homesickness, Bran and his faithful followers go back to Ireland, only to find that they have been away so long that they and their epic voyage are remembered only in the ancient legends. Bran departs and is never seen again.

The bowmen of Gwent, justifiably ranked among the greatest archers of all time, are also of old Celtic stock — the Welsh branch — and their warrior traditions go back many centuries. There is a strong possibility that the American Mandan bowmen may have acquired their skill from twelfth-century Welsh settlers led by Prince Madoc ap Owain Gwynedd.

When Owain Gwynedd died circa 1168, his sons quarrelled over the succession and young Prince Madoc was driven out by his brothers. He went into exile in North Wales where he decided to emigrate instead of fighting his brothers to regain his inheritance. He and a few loyal followers built a heavy cargo boat which they named the *Gwennan Corn*: a sturdy, full-bodied single-master. In 1169 or 1170, they launched her from a point near Conway on the Welsh coast and successfully crossed the Irish Sea and the Atlantic.

There is a plaque in Alabama — at Fort Morgan (an undeniably Welsh name!) — which records their landing in Mobile Bay in 1170. There are also three ancient fortified

---

[9] See T.F., O'Rahilly, *Early Irish History and Mythology*, 1946; Kuno Meyer, and Alfred Nutt, *The Voyage of Bran*, 1895; and G. and T Jones (translators), *The Mabinogion*, 1946.

[10] The term 'clew' refers to a ball of magic thread, or fine cord, of the kind which Ariadne used to guide Theseus out of the Cretan Labyrinth after he had slain the hideous bull-headed Minotaur.

buildings near Chattanooga in Tennessee which are built in
the early Welsh style. The unusually fair-haired Mandan
Indians once occupied the land alongside the Missouri
River, where they used small boats like Welsh coracles
instead of canoes. Tragically, most of the Mandans were
wiped out by a smallpox epidemic which fur traders
brought with them in 1838.

The most that can be said of Prince Madoc's legendary
voyage is that it is possible, even probable, but not proven
beyond a shadow of a doubt on the evidence currently available. If Madoc and his followers did reach Mobile Bay in
1170, it is not unreasonable to assume that they were well
aware of — and deliberately following — a long and honourable tradition of Celtic sea-rovers who had braved the
hazards of the Atlantic for centuries before them. Some of
those earlier expeditions might even have reached Nova
Scotia, and been responsible for the workings on Oak
Island. This argument is greatly strengthened by a comment from D. Morgan Rees, MA, FSA, Keeper of the
Department of Industry in the National Museum of Wales.
He writes:

> ... the evidence of applied industry during Roman times
> in Wales, and indeed earlier, has a fascination and pro-
> vides proof of great technical ability. The workings of the
> Dolaucothi goldmine the Ogofau, near Pumsaint,
> Carmarthenshire, and the meeting of their demands for
> water, provide proof of applied engineering of extraordi-
> narily high attainment. Some of the levels, which were
> driven into hillsides at this goldmine, may still be pene-
> trated to reveal their 'bold and regular workmanship'.
> The formation of roof and walls is such that it suggests,
> in some cases, that the level was driven so that loads
> could be carried hanging from yokes borne on human
> shoulders. That these levels were driven using only hand
> tools makes them all the more remarkable. An exception-
> al feature associated with this Roman goldmine was the
> watercourse, which brought water to it from a point on
> the river Cothi about seven miles away. It followed the
> steep hillside bounding the eastern side of the river valley
> running between the 600 and 800 feet contour lines.

Along part of its length continuity was only made possible
by cutting channels out of rock or a flat ledge into the
hillside. Despite the time which has elapsed, this aque-
duct may still be traced along part of its length enabling
it to be recognised as an outstanding feat of water engineering."[11]

Combining the underlying ideas found in the *imramha*
of early Celtic heroes (such as Bran the son of Febal) voyaging westward across the Atlantic, the twelfth-century references to Madoc ap Owain Gwynedd's epic journey, and the
skills of the Welsh miners who cut the Ogofau during
Roman times, produces a scenario equal to any theories
involving Drake, Kidd or Morgan.

Suppose a rich seam of gold is discovered in the Ogofau
during the fourth century. Roman power is declining and
control over Pumsaint and other distant parts of the
Empire is weakening. A powerful and far-sighted centurion
is in charge of the mine: less and less of its produce goes
back to Rome; more and more is stored secretly against the
coming barbarian storm from the north. Nowhere in
Britain is safe because of the deteriorating military and
political situation; legion after legion is being recalled to
Rome. It will be difficult for a former mine supervisor to go
home as an inexplicably rich man — and, in any case, the
crumbling Western Empire offers little or no security. His
Welsh miners tell of journeys across the Great Western
Ocean to blessed and happy lands. Perhaps he has even
met travellers who have returned safely from such journeys. His decision is made. With a shipload or two of
Roman legionaries, and the sturdy Welsh miners who cut
the Ogofau tunnels and their seven-mile waterway, our
centurion embarks with his Dolaucothi gold.

Could that Romano-Welsh party have reached Nova
Scotia and built themselves an underground labyrinth as a
combination of fortress and safe deposit? Did they live out

[11]R. Brinley Jones (Ed.), *Anatomy of Wales*, article entitled "Industry in Wales" by D. Morgan Rees, 86.
(Peterston-super-Ely, Glamorgan, Wales, Gwerin Publications, 1972.) See also D. Mercer, *Exploring Unspoilt
Britain* (London: Octopus Books, published for the National Trust, 1985), 56.

their lives on the shores of Mahone Bay, trade with the indigenous Americans and marry into local tribes which eventually absorbed them? It is not a theory that ranks highly on the scale of probability — but it is certainly not impossible.

From the Celts we proceed to the Norsemen: did Vikings construct the Money Pit? As James Enterline confirms in "Viking America"[12], Norse explorers followed the Celts northwards and westwards to Iceland, but to understand their motives for these journeys, we need to understand their characters and social organisation. Individualistic and isolationist by nature, the peoples of Denmark, Norway and Sweden, especially those living along the *viks* or *fjords* of the western coast of Scandinavia, were always keen to find more living space. Towards the end of the ninth century, Norse explorers found Iceland. At about the same time, Harald Fairhair set himself up as the first King of all Norway: an arrangement which angered many of the fiercely independent Vikings. Chieftains from the fjords, with their families and followers, headed away from Harald's authority to the freedom and opportunity offered by this new land to the north.

About a century later, Eirik Thorvaldsson, an Icelandic farmer and local chieftain, quarrelled with a neighbour over some borrowed agricultural equipment. When the feuding died down, Eirik was banished for three years, and sailed off with his family and followers to seek for new lands. He eventually reached Greenland and settled there. One of his colonists, Herjolf, had a devoted son, Bjarni, who came looking for him. Because of a navigational error, Bjarni and his crew missed Greenland altogether, but eventually sighted parts of north-eastern Canada, Nova Scotia or New England. They made three landings before locating Iceland, the Viking colony and Herjolf's farm.

As a result of hearing of Bjarni's adventures, Eirik's son, the famous Leif Eirikson, traced Bjarni's course in

---

[12] J. R. Enterline, *Viking America — The Norse Crossings and their Legacy*, (London: New English Library, 1973).

reverse and landed where he had done, naming the sites Helluland, Markland and Vinland respectively. Other voyagers included his brother, Thorvald, and a relative by marriage, Thorfinn the Valiant (Thorfinn Karlsefni) who had married the widow of Thorstein, Leif's elder brother.

The evidence for this Viking exploration of the Atlantic coasts of Canada and the U.S.A. in the early eleventh century is, therefore, very convincing indeed.[13]

The Viking scenario for Oak Island is comparable to the Romano-Welsh hypothesis. Given a group of skilful, fearless, independent but rather quarrelsome people, with a love of freedom and mastery of the sea, the arrival of Norse colonists in Mahone Bay is an undeniable possibility. But if Vikings dug the Money Pit and some at least of its ancillary workings, they are far more likely to have constructed it as a burial place for a great leader than as a treasure store. If, indeed, the Oak Island workings eventually turn out to be of Norse origin, the mysterious boxes which the drillers encountered are much more likely to be coffins than treasure chests. Could the 'loose metal' have been the remains of some type of early Norse chain mail?

Both Celts and Vikings would have had the skill, the strength, the organisation, the group discipline and the tenacity to have carried out the Oak Island work. They might also have had the opportunity. The historical question mark remains.

---

[13]See C.Gini , "The Location of Vinland", Papers of the Institute of Economics of the Norwegian School of Economics and Business Administration, Number 10, Bergen, 1958; and C.Gordon, *Before Columbus*,(New York, Crown, 1971)

13

RELIGIOUS REFUGEES

The original and challenging hypothesis outlined in this chapter came from the authors' good friend George Young, a very knowledgeable and experienced Nova Scotian surveyor, whose own excellent book on Oak Island is strongly recommended reading.[14] In addition to his valuable engineering and surveying background, George knows the world's seas and ocean currents from long, adventurous years of first-hand experience as a naval officer.

Born in Eastcote, Middlesex, England, in 1924, he added a couple of years to his age and joined the Royal Navy in 1940. Starting in a Naval Infantry Battalion, he transferred to destroyers, and was on loan to the Royal Canadian Navy for part of his active service career. He served aboard the *Montgomery* and *Georgetown,* then went to the frigate *Hargood* for the Normandy operations. After the war, he served as an officer in the Canadian Mercantile Marine on the West Indies and South American routes. During the Korean emergency, he again served as an officer in the Royal Canadian Navy.

In essence, George bases his ideas on his own special knowledge and experience of the sea and of the local Nova Scotian geology. He is also supported by Professor Barry

---

[14]George Young, *Ancient Peoples and Modern Ghosts* (Queensland, Halifax County, Nova Scotia, BOJ 1TO, 1980).

George Young with Patricia and Lionel Fanthorpe.

Fell's erudite translation of the mysterious stone found at, or near, the ninety-foot level by the Onslow team in 1803/4.

In the previous chapter, we considered the possibility that Celts or Vikings had created the Oak Island system: in the former case, perhaps, as a repository for Romano-Celtic gold from the Ogofau mine; in the latter case as a subterranean mausoleum for their leader. George Young's challenging theory directs our thoughts much farther to the south and east.

Basing his arguments on the strong likelihood that by the year 400 BC the early Amerindians were involved in trans-Atlantic trading with Carthaginians from the Mediterranean coasts, George uses his maritime expertise to plot their probable routes. His navigational arguments are sound and convincing. Passing the Pillars of Hercules (Gibraltar), one route followed by the Phoenician[15] and Carthaginian traders took them north along the Iberian coastline, around the Bay of Biscay and westwards along

[15]See for example, D.A Deal, *The Nexus*, (Columbus, Georgia: ISAC (Institute for the Study of American Cultures) Press, 1993), 124 – 127.

the English Channel to within sight of Cornwall. Keeping Ireland on their starboard side, they would head for the land they knew as Ogygia (Iceland). A westerly course would then take them past the southern tip of Greenland and Cape Race in Newfoundland. A turn to the south-west would bring them to Nova Scotia, and down the American Atlantic coast as far as Florida.

Their second feasible route would have taken them south-west of the Pillars of Hercules to the Canaries, where westerly flowing currents would ease their journey to Cuba and thence to Florida and so on up the American coast.

If they had begun their homeward journey from the vicinity of Cape Hatteras (North Carolina), George argues, they would have been able to make good use of the currents sweeping east again towards the Iberian Peninsula and the Pillars of Hercules — after which they would have been back in what were tantamount to home waters.

Another vital factor which lends considerable force to George's arguments is the change in the effective tidal levels which has taken place over the centuries. His studies have revealed that in the area around Mahone Bay and Oak Island, the water in Carthaginian times was thirty-five feet lower than it is now as a result of the coastal land masses settling down onto the Earth's crust at a rate of approximately eleven inches per century.

George hypothesises that a group of Mediterranean traders established a small permanent colony in Nova Scotia, in the neighbourhood of Martins Point, Western Shore and Gold River with a campsite at Beech Hill.

He surmises that they were a mixture of Phoenician and Greek stock, who would have written and spoken a version of Ptolemaic, a language indebted to both Greek and Arabic sources.

These pioneers would have noticed many of the natural limestone shafts and caverns in the area: ideal for adaptation as homes, storage areas and workshops. Tunnels could have been dug connecting cavern with cavern, and ventilator shaft with ventilator shaft. One very large, deep shaft in particular (today's Money Pit?) could have been dug to ventilate a gigantic cavern, far below the island.

George envisages the trading that would have gone on between the Mediterranean colonists and the Amerindians: the indigenous hunters exchanging furs and fresh meat for Mediterranean artifacts, timber and agricultural produce.

The last trader to visit the colony brings news of the savage and bitter war now raging back home in the Mediterranean between Rome and Carthage: the First Punic War fought from 264–41 BC Hundreds of their fine ocean-going ships have gone to the bottom, taking thousands of adventurous merchants and brave seamen with them. Their vital link with the Mediterranean severed, the colonists become increasingly dependent upon their Amerindian in-laws, and are slowly but surely subsumed, adjusting to nomadic life and abandoning their Oak Island base to dereliction and decay.

Old World causes frequently initiate New World consequences. It is now the fifth century AD. The Roman Empire itself has finally gone the same way as the Carthaginian

George Young pointing out the mysterious ancient campsite.

Empire which it had destroyed in 146 BC. In Egypt, there
was a religious conflict in the early Church between the
Greeks and the Copts. The latter were the descendants of
the original ancient Egyptians, and their language, too,
was directly derived from the original ancient Egyptian
language. The theological causes of the quarrel are too complex to be dealt with in detail at this point, but, essentially,
the Copts opposed the Council of Chalcedon in 450 AD while
the Greeks supported it. Professional mainstream theolo-
gians termed the Coptic beliefs *monophysite,* and the real
problem between them and the Greeks arose over their different understandings of the divine nature of Christ.
Chalcedonians believed in the "two-natures" theory of
Jesus — that He was both God and Man. Coptic mono-
physites preferred to think of Him as having only one
inseparable, Divine Nature.

At this point, the Vandals poured in from the East,
flooding over the wreckage of the Western Roman Empire
and driving a wave of pitiful refugees before them. George
believes that among these refugees was a party of singularly
determined and courageous Coptic Christians.

Some residual knowledge of the ancient Carthaginian
trans-Atlantic sea-routes must still have lingered among
the fifth-century Mediterranean traders: they would have
made optimum use of it in this emergency. The dangers of
the open sea were infinitely preferable to certain death at
the hands of the merciless Vandal conquerors.

According to George Young's intriguing theory, supported
by Professor Barry Fell's translation of the inscription
taken from the porphyry slab found in the Money Pit, a
boat load of Copts reached Nova Scotia and established
themselves there under the leadership of an *arif,* or "sub-
priest." When this revered Coptic leader died, those whom
he had led safely ahead of the Vandals, across the Atlantic,
and through the perilous pioneering days of establishing
their settlement, would have wanted to show their respect
and gratitude. No labour would have been too great to
ensure that his precious remains rested in peace. These

were men who had seen the pyramids and knew something of the intricate protective devices they contained to thwart grave-robbers. Would they have done less for their arif than the Pharaohs' architects and artificers had done for their ancient god-kings?

But how is George's bold, avant-garde theory to be reconciled with various other Oak Island findings such as Nolan's enigmatic markers, the puzzling core samples, the chests (or coffins?) which the drillers were so confident they had encountered at around ninety to 100 feet in 1849 (and which Blair's team may have re-encountered between 150 and 170 feet nearly fifty years later)? And what about the apparent difficulties posed by Triton's radio-carbon dating tests?

It is possible to construct several strong bridges between George's ideas and those previously established facts. A party of religious refugees escaping from Egypt would not necessarily have been averse to taking with them such treasures as were accessible to them. The Israelites set a classic precedent during the Exodus: they took a vast store of Egyptian treasure with them.[16] The engraved porphyry slab found between the eighty- and ninety- foot levels in 1803–4 also gives a strong hint of Egyptian origins.

There can be no certainty that all the complex workings below Oak Island were made by the same people at the same time. A pre-Christian colony of Carthaginian traders, followed by Coptic refugees who might have heard legends and old tales of what their predecessors had accomplished, could well account for a second elaborate subterranean structure being superimposed upon an earlier one. A difference in sea-level of over thirty feet would have made their task far easier than the daunting excavationary work confronting nineteenth- and twentieth-century explorers.

 ·Careful burial beneath oak platforms, clay seals, coconut fibre and charcoal is reminiscent of the meticulous protective processes which guarded high-ranking Egyptian

---

[16]Exod. 12: 35, 36

dead. Copts would have been familiar with all of this. Water tunnels and flood-traps to drown grave-robbers have much in common with the ancient Nile culture which jealously protected its dead by every means that human ruthlessness and ingenuity could devise.

George has also made a highly significant breakthrough in a totally different field, a discovery which will provide a wealth of valuable research material for Oak Island and Rennes-le-Château investigators for many years to come. "Only connect," as E. M. Forster said on the title page of *Howard's End*. Having studied the Poussin paintings carefully because he shared our interest in the Rennes mystery, and having a detailed knowledge of the ancient Ogham alphabet, George suddenly noticed that many of the characters portrayed on Poussin's canvases have their hands painted in what appear to be Ogham alphabet signs.

The Ogham alphabet is the oldest form of Goidelic, a Celtic dialect. Like all truly great codes and cyphers, its power lies in its simplicity. A vertical or horizontal line has

George Young and Patricia Fanthorpe studying the Ogham letters on the Poussin canvases.

one, two, three or more shorter lines branching out from it at right-angles to represent letters. These branches can be left or right of a vertical line, or above or below a horizontal line. They are, therefore, ideally suited for use as hand signals. In theory at least, two competent Ogham users could communicate in this sign language without a sound being uttered. Was it used, perhaps, by early Irish monks under vows of silence? Or by prisoners trying to pass secret messages which their jailers must not hear? If Nicholas Poussin (1593–1665) was the master of priceless coded secrets which many Rennes researchers believe him to have been, then his hitherto unsuspected trump card must surely have been his knowledge of the Ogham script, and his incredibly cunning use of it in the hand signals of his shepherds, the shepherdess and other characters.

There is an enigmatic inscription below a carving in the grounds of Shugborough Hall, Staffordshire, England. That carving depicts a reversed copy of Poussin's Arcadian shepherds. The strange inscription ("O_U_O_S_V_A_V_V" with a "D_" and an "M_" immediately to the left and right of it on the line below) may have a very significant new interpretation when George Young's discovery of the Ogham letters displayed by the shepherds' stone hands are added to it.

Shugborough Hall is significant, first because it was the ancestral home of the Anson family, whose founder, William Anson, was a successful lawyer, a contemporary of Sir Francis Bacon during the period of his political ascendancy. (Bacon's possible connection with the Oak Island mystery is treated in detail in chapter 16.) The second connection is through Admiral George Anson (1697–1762), a descendant of William's, who came home immensely rich from his round-the-world voyage in the *Centurion*, 1740–1744. Remembering the possible William Kidd connection with the China or *Chene* (Oak?) Sea, it is interesting to note that Admiral Anson's *Centurion* was the first British warship to enter the China Sea when he sailed to Canton to sell the

Shugborough Hall in Staffordshire.

The Shepherd's Monument at Shugborough Hall.

treasure he had taken from the Spaniards. Admiral Anson may have yet another connection with the Oak Island Money Pit, and it has to do with a possible political conspiracy at the very highest level.

George III (1738–1820) struggled long and hard to regain many of the old, lost royal powers. He did not wish to be a puppet or figurehead at the mercy of various powerful Ministers of the Crown. Charles I's struggles against his parliament a century before had failed more for financial than for political or religious reasons. If Charles had had adequate funding, the British Civil War might well have gone the other way. George was determined not to repeat Charles's error, but how could he become financially independent of his Government? Suppose that a very small *clique* of trusted royalists including Anson had planned the raid on Havana in 1762 (the year of Anson's death while still serving as a highly placed member of the Board of Admiralty). Suppose that there were not merely a few hundred thousand pounds — as officially reported taken from Havana — but many millions, which only George III's clique knew anything about. Was this secret surplus intended to become George III's private royal reserve? Was Anson in on the plot before his death and did the bulk of that 'missing' Havana treasure find its way to the Oak Island labyrinth? It is yet another perfectly reasonable theory, and it provides one more strange link in the circuitous, circumstantial chain shackling Shugborough Hall to the ancient Arcadian treasure, to Poussin's paintings and to the Ogham script. That Ogham script now leads back again to George Young in Nova Scotia.

The famous, but controversial, Mount Hanley Stone, discovered by Edward Hare and examined by George Young in 1983, is about a metre long and covered with curious markings which look uncommonly like an ancient Ogham inscription. So where do all these curious discoveries point?

For the sake of argument, let's assume that the ancient and mysterious Arcadian treasure really exists — whatever form it may take. Some of its ancient guardians were familiar with both forms of the Ogham script — they could use it as a hand alphabet for secret, silent signalling, and they could also write, paint or carve it. When written or carved, its very simplicity helped to keep it concealed: casual observers could so easily mistake it for accidental or natural markings. Only a searcher who knew what he or she was looking for would be able to locate and decipher it. Poussin hid Ogham letters and other strange clues in his paintings. Thousands of people studied those canvases for centuries before George Young's perceptiveness and intuition revealed the Ogham letters. Another ancient secret-sharer hid clues at Glozel on the weird engraved clay tablets which Fradin found there in 1924. Shugborough Hall has indirect links via William Anson with Francis Bacon and his elder brother, Anthony, who was engaged on secret service activities in Europe. Shugborough's grounds contain the Shepherd Monument, reflecting Poussin's characters displaying their Ogham letters in stone.

An even stranger parallel link in this weird chain is forged by those other masters of secret codes and cyphers: the indomitable Templars. How much did they know of the Arcadian treasure and its possible journey to Oak Island?

14

THE INDOMITABLE
TEMPLARS

The Templars' full Latin name was *pauperes commili-tones Christi templique Salomonici:* the Poor Knights of Christ and of the Temple of Solomon. In 1119 Godfroi de St Omer and Hugues de Payns of Burgundy went to Jerusalem with the stated intention of giving up worldly chivalry, living in poverty, chastity and obedience, fighting for the true and supreme King (Christ) and guarding the public roads so that pilgrims could travel in safety. Six other knights joined them. Baldwin II, who was King of Jerusalem from 1118–31, gave the Templars part of his palace. This area was close to the al-Aksa Mosque, which was popularly referred to as Solomon's Temple. From that location the order took its name.

Graham Hancock in *The Sign and the Seal*[17] makes some very interesting and well-researched alternative historical suggestions about the earliest days of the Templars. In his view, the nine original founders (not eight!) went to the Temple site for a completely different purpose. Hancock points out with a fair degree of logic that eight or nine knights would have been hopelessly inadequate defenders over the many miles of road that the pilgrims had to cover. The Order would need to grow significantly before it could

---

[17]Graham Hancock, *The Sign and the Seal* (London: Heinemann, 1992).

function as an effective defence force.

In Hancock's opinion, the founders of the Order went to the supposed site of Solomon's Temple to excavate beneath it for lost secrets and hidden treasures — much the same reason that Bérenger Saunière had for acquiring the living of Rennes-le-Château some seven centuries later.[18] Perhaps the original Templars suspected that the Ark of the Covenant had been concealed in a secret cave below Solomon's Temple before the city fell. Perhaps it was the Holy Grail they hoped to retrieve.

It may well have been that they were searching for something even older and more mysterious — something which might also have been called the Grail, the Greal or the Gral, but was not the traditional Cup which Christ used at the Last Supper. Was it something which had left Egypt at the time of the Exodus and been carefully preserved by Solomon the Wise, one of the very few *illuminati* who recognized it for what it really was and who understood at least part of its proper use and its potentially immense powers?

During their earliest period, the Templars wore no special uniform, habit or dress, and they seemed genuinely poor. They were also very much an evangelical and redemptive order. Part of their function was to look for former knights who had fallen from grace and failed to live up to the high standards expected of them. For these excommunicated men they sought absolution, and then welcomed them into their Order as fellow Templars.

Bernard of Clairvaux (1090–1153), like Hugues de Payns, was a member of the Burgundian nobility. He was a curiously shy and timid boy, even during his education by the Canons of St. Vorles at Chatillon, although he gained there the reputation of being a young literary genius.

The death of his beloved mother, Aleth, when he was only seventeen, had a profound effect on Bernard's life. Richly gifted with the power of objective self-appraisal, he

---

[18]R.L. and P.A .Fanthorpe, *Secrets of Rennes-le-Château* (York Beach, Maine: Samuel Weiser Inc., 1992).

despised his own weakness and timidity and decided to do something drastic and dramatic to put it right. The very strict Benedictine Monastery at Citeaux had recently been opened, and Bernard told his family that it was his intention to go there. Not surprisingly, they tried to dissuade him. The results were almost incredible. It was the quiet, shy, timid Bernard who persuaded some thirty of them to join him at Citeaux! In 1115 Abbot Stephen Harding sent him to Champagne to found the Abbey of Clairvaux. All through his life he had this same amazing charisma and power to persuade: yet it was the last characteristic that anyone who met him would have expected from such a shy, withdrawn, self-effacing and solitary man. His influence on the politics, the theology and the monastic organisation of his day was incalculable. He was 'the conscience of Europe' in the twelfth century, and he was a conscience who had the power to direct the mighty. Popes, kings and princes all responded to his massive influence.

Needless to say, he was a key force in the establishment of the Knights Templar. Bernard himself wrote that Israel at that time was infested with "rogues, impious men, robbers, committers of sacrilege, murderers, perjurers and adulterers." The Templars reclaimed this human flotsam and jetsam and gave them a worthwhile purpose in life. In consequence, like the French Foreign Legion some seven centuries later, the Templars were characterized by their strength and determination and an independence of spirit that other soldiers envied. They were rugged and free: honour mattered more to them than life. Not for nothing did they choose their well-deserved motto and battle cry: "First to attack and last to retreat!"

Freedom from excommunication by any local clergy — mere Parish Priests and Bishops — gave the Templars a clear edge over most other organisations. In twelfth century Christendom, the fear of excommunication was taken seriously. It kept many a tyrant in check. Like their symbol, the chess board knight, the Templars were free to 'jump' over administrative, political and religious barriers that blocked most others. Like a multi-national company in the modern world of high finance, their Order could laugh at most state Governments.

Bernard of Clairvaux gave the Templars his invaluable support in 1127 in *De laude novae militiae*. The Council of Troyes recognized them officially in 1128.

Yet there remains a dark shadow to cloud these shining ideals. Historians have argued long and hard over whether there was a secret rule which the Templars followed, as well as their widely publicised open rule, rendered in French as *Règle du Temple*.

Adventurers who travelled as the Templars did, inevitably came into contact with Eastern civilisations and the strange secrets they nurtured. Much esoteric Eastern wisdom undoubtedly came the Templars' way, and undoubtedly they treasured it and made the most of it. They also came into contact with Byzantium and the ancient knowledge that had flourished there for over a thousand years.

Templars were like war-canoes that flourished amid the white water of frequent battles. When the tides of war crash over ancient cities, secrets that have lain safely hidden for centuries tend to get exposed. A bastion falls here. A tower crumbles there. Secret rooms and hiding places are revealed to the light like the egg chambers of ants' nests when a plough goes through them.

Many Templars were rough and ready soldiers of fortune who had been reformed and restored by the Order. Who knows what they might have pillaged here, there and everywhere in the past — only to bring it to their central treasury once they had re-started their lives. An isolated piece of jigsaw is meaningless; but bring a score such pieces together and some proto-idea of the picture may begin to crystallise. Combine a yarn from Damascus with a souvenir from Alexandria; link a legend from Cyprus with a fable from Eschol; add a curio from Cairo to a keepsake from Thebes: let the travelling adventurers talk long into the night around their campfire at Damietta. Who knows what intricate patterns may emerge?

Most significant of all was Templar acquisition of ancient Egyptian knowledge. Egypt was the traditional home of the secret Hermetic texts, the ancient home of Thoth (otherwise known as Hermes Trismegistus), author and wielder of the famous Emerald Tablets of Power.[19] If there was a Secret Order of the Templars — and its existence is probable rather than merely possible — then it is equally likely to have been the twelfth century human repository of the ancient hermetic secrets, and, in particular, of the greatest of all the Hermetic Treasures: the Emerald Tablets of Trismegistus.

Bernard of Clairvaux, the great power behind the Templars, died in 1153, but long before they lost him, the Templars were well established in practically every Christian Kingdom — even, perhaps, in the semi-legendary Kingdom of Prester John.

Who was Prester John? Legends of him began in the twelfth century with the arrival in Rome in 1122, during the pontificate of Calixtus II, of a Church official from India (or the Indies) an area frequently confused with Abyssinia and Ethiopia. Tales grew that Prester John had a massive Christian power base in the Far East and would appear at any moment to assist the Crusaders in their struggles against the Saracens — rather like King Arthur in Britain or Good King Wenceslas in Bohemia, who are both said to be sleeping, ready to appear in their lands' hour of need.

The first written comment on Prester John seems to be in the chronicle of Bishop Otto of Freisingen. Otto tells of a visit he made to the Papal Court in 1145 where he met the Bishop of Gabala (which was probably Jibal in Syria). This Syrian church leader told Otto about Prester John, who ruled a Kingdom well to the east of Media and Persia. It was said that John, who was a good Christian but a Nestorian,[20] had fought his neighbours and beaten them soundly, then headed for the Tigris to assist his western

---

[19]Lewis Spence, *The Encyclopedia of the Occult* (London: Bracken Books, 1988), 143.
[20]Nestorius (circa 380 – 451), Patriarch of Constantinople from 428 to 431, argued against the use of the term Θεοτοκος (Mother of God) to describe Mary the Mother of Jesus. See J.F. Bethune-Baker, *Nestorius and his Teaching,*, 1908.

brethren against the Saracens. Unfortunately, he had been unable to cross it, and had gone home again.

In 1165 a letter went into wide circulation describing Prester John's amazing kingdom, his invincible armies and his untold wealth. A second letter — this time attributed to Pope Alexander III — went out on September 22nd, 1177: no less than 55 years on from the first rumours of Prester John's existence! The gist of this epistle was that Pope Alexander had heard of Prester John via the Papal Physician, Philip, who had in turn received the information from "honourable members of that Monarch's Kingdom" whom he had met in eastern lands. In response to John's various requests for a church in Jerusalem, and other privileges, Alexander III advised him that humility would bring these great rewards sooner than vaunting pride.

Further confusion arose during the thirteenth century with persistent rumours of a great new army from the east attacking the Moslems. Unfortunately these newcomers turned out to be the Mongol hordes of Jenghiz Khan (1162–1227) rather than Prester John's long-awaited Christian reinforcements.

Christian travellers in India and the east tried to find a local potentate on whom the title of Prester John could reasonably be conferred. In 1248 Carpini described him as the Christian King of India. Rubruquis in 1253 thought that Prester (or King, as he called him) John was in reality Kushluk, ruler of the Naimans, who was the brother of Ung Khan, Jenghiz's ally. Marco Polo says that this same "Unc Khan" [sic] was Lord of the Tartars until Jenghiz rose to power. At about the same time, the peripatetic Friar John of Montecorvino was authoring reports that Prester John's descendants held territory in Kuku Khotan (about 500 km north of present day Peking). Odoric, another friar, supported John of Montecorvino's accounts, but after their time the Asian stories petered out, and the reported location of Prester John's Kingdom shifted to Africa.[21]

---

[21] For information on Prester John see: Friedrich Zarncke, *Der Priester Johannes* (Leipzig: 1870); M. d'Averac, "Recueil de Voyages et de Memoires" in *Societe de Geographie*, volume iv, 547–564, Paris, 1839).

As historians and researchers wend their way cautiously through the myths and legends concerning Prester John, one or two solid and highly significant facts begin to emerge. Fra Mauro's wonderful map of 1549 situates a great city in Abyssinia with the words: "Here is Prester John's principal residence." From 1481–1495 King John II of Portugal was sending missions to Africa to try to establish communications with Prester John, and Vasco da Gama was certainly convinced that Prester John's Kingdom was somewhere in that continent.[22]

To obtain the first clear perspective on the facts relating to Prester John and his mysterious kingdom, it is necessary to go back nearly two millennia before the Prester's era and examine the account of the visit of the Queen of Sheba to the Court of King Solomon.[23] R.S. Poole, an authoritative academic writer on the staff of the British Museum in the nineteenth century, makes out an interesting case for identifying the Kingdom of Seba (or Sheba) with Ethiopia rather than an Arabian kingdom. He also points out that the proper names of the first and second kings of the Ethiopian Twenty-fifth Dynasty of Egypt were Shebek and Shebetek. In the Biblical list of patriarchs and tribal founders, Seba is shown to be the son of Cush (Noah's grandson) which also makes him brother to Nimrod 'the mighty hunter.' Poole argues that these ancient Cushite kingdoms extended throughout the Arabian Peninsula and down into North Africa.[24]

An ancient Ethiopian document, the *Kebra Nagast* (which means "The Kings' Glory")[25] gives a clear account of the relationship between Solomon and Makeda, the Queen of Sheba, and its sequel. It is related that their son, Menelik (which means "Son of the Wise Man") eventually took the Ark of the Covenant to Ethiopia and became the

---

[22]Gustav Oppert, *Der Presbyter Johannes in Sage und Geschichte* (Berlin: 1870)

[23]1 Kings 10 vv 1–13, repeated in 2 Chron. 9: 1–12

[24]William Smith, (Ed.), *A Dictionary of the Bible, Volume 3*, article entitled "Seba" by R.S Poole, 1188–9.
There is also interesting support for this idea in Ps. 252: 10: "The kings of Sheba and Seba shall offer gifts."

[25]G. Hancock, *The Sign and the Seal* (London: Mandarin Paperbacks, 1993), 44.

first of the great dynasty which lasted until the tragic over-
throw of Emperor Haile Selassie in 1974. In this Ethiopian
tradition, each local Church contains a replica of the Ark
known as a *tabot*, but, surprisingly, these replicas are flat
tablets and not, as would naturally be expected, box-shaped
containers. The Ethiopians themselves believe that the
original Ark is now preserved in safety and secrecy in the
city of Axum. How does all this link up with the Templars?

Chartres Cathedral in France had beautiful Gothic
additions made to it between 1194 and 1225. The carvings
then made on both its north and south porches include the
Queen of Sheba. On the north porch she is shown next to
Solomon, and accompanied by an African attendant.[26]
These Gothic carvings are contemporary with the mysterious old Ethiopian document, the *Kebra Nagast* — and with
Wolfram von Eschenbach's *Parzival*. which tells of a young
knight's extensive travels and strange adventures during
his quest for the Holy Grail. One episode relates how the
handsome young knight, Gahmuret of Anjou, travels to distant Zazamanc and has a love affair with its beautiful
black queen Belacane. A son, Feirefiz, is born as a result of
their union. He grows up to become a great warrior hero.
Inexplicably, Gahmuret leaves the exquisite Belacane,
returns to Europe and marries Herzeloyde by whom he has
another son. This second boy grows up to become Parzival
himself, the hero of the Grail saga which bears his name.
The inference must be drawn that the early thirteenth-century sculptors at Chartres were taking their instructions
from someone who knew of the Ethiopian tradition contained in the *Kebra Nagast,* and of the strange parallels
between Solomon's love for Makeda, Queen of Sheba, and
Gahmuret's affair with the lovely Belacane.

It is not only the mysterious porch carvings which make
Chartres Cathedral such an interesting field for historical
research. The whole design, structure and layout of this
arcane building is a mathematical miracle. One viable
explanation is that part of what the Templars found hidden

---

[26]Song of Sol. 1: 5–6.

beneath what they believed to be Solomon's Temple were a number of ancient and esoteric building and design secrets. These were duly made available to the Chartres builders. For the Ethiopian secrets contained in the *Kebra Nagast* to have reached Chartres as well, there must also have been Templar representatives at the Ethiopian Court of the monarch who had inherited the mantle of 'Prester John.' This would seem to have been King Lalibela, whose early infancy provides yet another mysterious link with Rennes-le-Château and the Arcadian Treasure. A prodigious swarm of bees surrounded his cradle and his mother called out "Lalibela!" which meant literally that the bees recognized his supremacy.[27] The bee was also a vitally important Merovingian symbol, and the Merovingians are inextricably intertwined with the Arcadian Treasure of Rennes. King Childeric's burial place, for example, held a 'swarm' of 300 golden bees surrounding the royal body.[28]

How does all of this now begin to come together? In the Ethiopian tradition, Solomon's son by Sheba is Menelik, founder of the Dynasty. He makes a secret expedition to Israel, where his royal father recognizes and honours him. When he returns to Ethiopia the Ark of the Covenant and its precious contents are with him. He also has loyal Jewish companions who follow him partly because he is Solomon's son, and partly to serve as guardians of the Ark. Did they become the founders of the Ethiopian Jewish community, the Falashas?

That there were various sharply divided political factions in Israel at that time is made clear in Biblical history by the account of the rebellion led by Jeroboam son of Nebat, a revolutionary who had strong links with Egypt.[29]

It has already been demonstrated that the Ethiopian *tabots* are tablets, or flattish cuboids, rather than boxes or containers. In Parzival the Grail is described as a stone,

---

[27] Sergew Hable-Selassie, *Ancient and Medieval Ethiopian History to 1270* (Addis Ababa: Haile-Selassie I University, 1972), 265.

[28] M. Baigent, R. Leigh, H.Lincoln, *The Holy Blood and the Holy Grail* (London: Jonathan Cape, 1982), Corgi Paperback Edition, 248.

[29] 2 Chron. 9:31– 2 Chron. 10:19.

rather than a drinking vessel.[30] The statue of the mighty and mysterious Melchizedek at Chartres shows him holding a cup which contains a stone.

So a new scenario begins. Suppose that something of that shape, something of immense power and value, once made its way from ancient Egypt to Israel and eventually at least part of it went from Solomon's Temple to Ethiopia, the 'Kingdom of Prester John.' Knowledge of that priceless mystery reached the ears of the Templars. Wolfram encoded some of its secret history in Parzival. Informed by the Templars, the builders at Chartres encoded more of it in stone. The Templars took possession of it, or, perhaps that part of it which complements something which is preserved so carefully at Axum. Did the Templars remove the priceless contents from the Ark, while leaving the Ark itself in Ethiopia?

Then came the Templar tragedy. Philip IV of France betrayed the Order and did his best to destroy it in 1307. Happily, he did not quite succeed. The noble Sinclairs of Orkney sheltered and protected the Templar refugees, who were by no means ungrateful to their valiant hosts. With Sinclair support and Zeno navigational skills, a party of Templars crossed the North Atlantic and reached Nova Scotia. Did they carry the Grail Stones, or Tablets, with them?

The knowledge of engineering design that built Chartres Cathedral would have been more than enough to plan and excavate the Oak Island Money Pit and the labyrinth beneath. Andrew Sinclair's scrupulously researched and systematically constructed study of the Templars' movements after 1307[31] lends massive weight to Mike Bradley's excellent earlier study.[32] Crooker and Nolan's fascinating discoveries on Oak Island, described in detail in "Oak Island Gold,"[33] also point inescapably to

---

[30] Wolfram von Eschenbach, *Parzival*, translated by H.M. Mustard, and C.E. Passage (New York: 1961), 251.

[31] Andrew Sinclair, *The Sword and the Grail* (London: Random House, 1993).

[32] Michael Bradley, *Holy Grail Across the Atlantic* (Toronto: Hounslow Press, 1988).

[33] William S. Crooker, *Oak Island Gold* (Halifax, Nova Scotia: Nimbus Publishing, 1993).

Templar involvement. We were also privileged to see a pre-liminary draft manuscript of Bill Mann's forthcoming vol-ume (on which he sought our advice). His excellent research and exciting conclusions will make this a highly significant work, one which will shed light on the Rennes-le-Château mystery and will powerfully reinforce Sinclair and Bradley's intriguing Templar theories.[34]

When a secret is as important as that which the Templars found and protected, two vital criteria arise: first, it must be guarded as strongly as possible against unwel-come intruders; secondly, it must never be lost. There is a dilemma and a paradox here. 'Spare keys' must be kept, but they must also be so carefully concealed that they can-not be found accidentally by the 'wrong' people.

Were those keys to be found in Poussin's paintings? Are vital clues preserved in the carvings outside Shugborough Hall? In the curious manuscripts which Bérenger Saunière found at Rennes-le-Château? In the weird alphabet that young Fradin dug up at Glozel near Vichy in 1924? Part of the solution to the Oak Island mystery may still lie con-cealed in a Merovingian mausoleum below the Church of St Mary Magdalene in Rennes-le-Château, where the enig-matic Father Saunière was once Parish Priest.

---

[34]William F. Mann, *Nova Scotia: The New Jerusalem*

Saunière's painting of St. Mary Magdalene.

Interior of the ruined Château Hautpoul at Rennes-le-Château.

15

THE FRENCH CONNECTION: RENNES AND GLOZEL

Rennes-le-Château has deservedly been described as one of the most mysterious places on earth and a 'gateway to the invisible.' This remote, hilltop village certainly has a strange air of unreality, a unique atmosphere which is redolent of the arcane and the esoteric.

Its chequered history extends over several millennia. The ancient artifacts which Monsieur Fatin, the sculptor, showed us in the store rooms of his crumbling Château Hautpoul, go right back to the Stone Age. He found them all in and around Rennes. Celtic Tectosages once settled here, a tribe whose very name meant 'The Wise Builders.' The Romans were here, and very much in evidence at Rennes-les-Bains just across the valley. It was here in Rennes-les-Bains that secretive and scholarly old Father Boudet studied the ancient Celtic language and the timeless cromlechs near his village. At neighbouring Coustaussa, the tapering stone fingers of another ruined *château* point enigmatically to the silent sky. Most curious of all is the nearby site of the Tomb of Arques. This amazing place once held vital clues to the Arcadian Treasure. The authors visited the tomb in 1975, heaved up its cracked stone lid and photographed the dark mystery below. The tomb as it stood then was a perfect replica of the tomb which Poussin had depicted on his canvas of the Arcadian Shepherds.

M. Fatin the sculptor, owner of Château Hautpoul.

Stone-age artifacts from M. Fatin's collection.

The village of Coustaussa viewed from the cemetery where Father Gélis lies.

Patricia Fanthorpe in the doorway of mysterious old Father Boudet's church in
Rennes-les-Bains.

Rennes and its area are surrounded by other mysteries as well as the Arcadian tomb, many of them sinister and tragic. Old Father Gélis of Coustaussa was brutally murdered with an axe, a century ago. His killer was never caught. There were many mysterious aspects to the crime. The suspicious old man would open the door of his presbytery to no one but his niece when she brought him his meals and clean linen. He insisted that she remain on the doorstep until he had re-bolted the door after taking in the supplies she had brought him. Despite all these elaborate precautions, someone, or something, got into the house and battered the old man to death. The brutal savagery of the killing left bloodstains everywhere, yet there was no trace of the murderer's foot or handprint.

Bérenger Saunière was born in Couiza Montazels, just across the valley from Rennes-le-Château. Those who knew him best as a child said that while other children played their normal games, young Bérenger would lead his adventurous boyhood companions into the woods and rocky valleys around Rennes and say: "Let us go and search for the lost treasure."

He grew up strong and athletic, a powerful, independent, ambitious man, who hardly seemed cut out for the priesthood. Yet he endured long, boring years of seminary deprivation and discipline in order to complete his rigorous theological and pastoral training. Did Bérenger Saunière have a genuine vocation? God alone can judge a question as significant as that: no human arbiter should ever presume to do so. The possibility remains, however, that he put up with it all simply to gain access to Rennes-le-Château and its ancient Church of St. Mary Magdalene. Just imagine that from his earliest youth, someone knowledgeable and influential during his vital formative years had convinced young Saunière that there was an ancient treasure — the fabulous Arcadian treasure — hidden at Rennes. He was a determined character, and a shrewd one. What better vantage point than the Presbytery of Rennes? What better local authority than that of the village Priest? Was that why Saunière did it? But there may have been still more to it than that: the Saunière family of Couiza-Montazels went back a long way. That area of south-western France had once been the territory of the independent Counts of Razes. It had strong Merovingian connections. It had once been Cathar and Templar heartland. Pedigrees went back for centuries, and local families were proud of their ancient lineages. The noble Hautpoul family had once owned the *château* which gave Rennes-le-Château its name. The ruined Château Blanchefort nearby was once said to have been a Templar stronghold, and there was another legendary Templar citadel at Bézu.

What if the impressionable young Saunière had been led to believe (rightly or wrongly) that he had Merovingian blood in his veins, that he was descended from the same Dagobert II who featured in the legend of the Arcadian treasure, or from the Counts of Razes — that he was, in fact, as far as anyone could be in the nineteenth century, the rightful and legitimate heir of those who had concealed the Arcadian treasure at Rennes so many centuries ago?

A picture begins to emerge. Saunière obtains the living of Rennes-le-Château. Within a matter of months he is indisputably one of the wealthiest men in the south of France. He spends money like water until his death — in suspicious circumstances — in 1917. What was the source of his sudden wealth?

Once again, the trail goes back to Solomon, and earlier still. Saunière is said in one account of the mystery to have had access to certain secret documents, which were found in his church. When these were decoded they alluded to a treasure that had once been in Sion (Jerusalem), and had eventually passed from there to the Merovingian King Dagobert II.

Much further back in the mists of time Melchizedek was priest-king of Salem (Jerusalem?) when he met Abraham the Patriarch.[35] The concept of a priest-king is an inescapable reminder of the title of the elusive Prester

---

[35]Gen. 14:18

John and his connection with Solomon's lineage.

Suppose that the ancient Arcadian treasure (whatever it actually was) had been known both to the ancient Egyptian Pharaohs as well as to Melchizedek, and that it had travelled as a unit, or perhaps in instalments, from Egypt to Salem — or even in the reverse direction. Ancient Jewish legends tell of Sarah (Abraham's sister-wife) encountering the sleeping Hermes Trismegistus (alias Thoth? alias Melchizedek?) in a cavern during the long journeys which she and Abraham undertook. The legend says that she disturbed the fabulous Emerald Tablets and that the sleeper began to stir. Sarah fled from the cave without them.

Long years pass. The Israelites have gone to Egypt as honoured guests — the family of Joseph, saviour of starving Egypt. They have left centuries later as runaway slaves under the protecting hand of Yahweh and the guidance of his servant Moses. Pharaoh does something that is tanta-mount to military insanity: he hurls the best of his chario-teers in reckless pursuit of the Israelites across a very dangerous stretch of temporarily dry land — until very recently the bed of the Red Sea. The waters rush back. The cream of Pharaoh's horsemen are destroyed. The triumphant Israelites escape. So why did Pharaoh do it? What motivated this particular piece of tactical lunacy, the Egyptian equivalent of the suicidal Charge of the Light Brigade in the Crimean War as immortalised in the poem by Tennyson (first published in *The Examiner* on December 9, 1854)?

When the Israelites left Egypt, they did not leave empty handed. Were part of the treasures they carried with them the priceless Emerald Tablets of Hermes Trismegistus, and did those fabulous Emerald Tablets eventually form the core of the legendary Arcadian treasure associated with Rennes-le-Château? Rennes-le-Château was deep in Cathar country, barely half-a-day's ride from the great Cathar fortress of Montségur. When the four fearless Cathar mountaineers escaped from that last fatal siege in 1244 carrying *"pecuniam infinitam"* and "the treasures of their faith," did the Emerald Tablets go with them? Was it the indomitable Templars who took over where the defeated Cathars left off? Did part of that Arcadian treasure make its way to a secret repository in a hidden Merovingian mausoleum deep beneath the ancient Church of St. Mary Magdalene at Rennes? When the Templars themselves went down in 1307, did the Arcadian treasure leave an ungrateful European mainland and find safety with the noble House of Sinclair in the Orkneys? Did some, at least, of the Emerald Tablets go from Rennes to Oak Island with the Templar refugees and the Zeno navigators?

And what of Nicholas Poussin's place in the strange tale of Rennes and the Arcadian treasure? How does he provide a link connecting Admiral Anson of Shugborough Hall, the shepherds and shepherdess at the Tomb of Arques and the coded parchments which Bérenger Saunière was said to have discovered in his church?

During the heyday of the opulent Louis XIV, the so-called Sun King of France (1638–1715), Nicholas Fouquet, his minister of finance, had a younger brother who acted as one of his espionage agents. This younger Fouquet met Poussin, the painter, in Italy. Vitally important secret information passed between them. Fouquet junior wrote a very excited letter home to Nicholas, his elder brother, the massive power-behind-the-throne, often referred to by historians as 'the real King of France.' Amazingly that letter has survived in French archives:

> I have given to Monsieur Poussin the letter that you were kind enough to write to him; he displayed overwhelming joy on receiving it. You wouldn't believe, sir, the trouble that he takes to be of service to you, or the affection with which he goes about this, or the talent and integrity that he displays at all times.
>
> He and I have planned certain things of which in a little while I shall be able to inform you fully; things which will give you, through M. Poussin, advantages which kings would have great difficulty in obtaining from

him, and which, according to what he says, no-one in the
world will ever retrieve in the centuries to come ... and
they are matters so difficult to enquire into that nothing
on earth at the present time could bring a greater fortune
nor, perhaps, ever its equal."[36]

Shortly afterwards, Fouquet senior fell from power, and
has long been one of the leading candidates proposed by
research historians for the unenviable role of The Man in
the Iron Mask. This unfortunate character was held at various prisons in top security conditions, and ended his days
in the Bastille itself. No one except St. Mars, the Governor
and totally trusted agent of Louis XIV, was ever allowed to
communicate with the mysterious masked prisoner. When
he finally died, all furniture from his cell was destroyed,
and the walls themselves were stripped and re-plastered.

Only one rational explanation for his weird behaviour
seems to present itself. The masked prisoner was so well-
known (as Fouquet was) that his face must not be seen in
case influential friends attempted to free him. If he held a
secret (one that Poussin had given him?) which made him
potentially so dangerous that he was a threat to the throne
itself, he must never be allowed to escape, nor to communicate with his powerful family, friends and allies outside.

So why not simply kill so dangerous a rival? Louis XIV
had few moral inhibitions. Removing a threat by liquidating
an opponent would not have troubled the royal conscience
unduly. The dangerous masked prisoner would have been
kept alive only because the King himself wanted the captive's priceless secret. Fouquet — if it was Fouquet — was
also a wily politician, who understood the vagaries and
vicissitudes of power only too well. Life was sweet — even
as a masked prisoner. Fouquet would not part with
Poussin's Arcadian Secret (assuming that he'd got it)
because he knew that the moment he did he would be murdered on Louis's order. It was a classical Mexican stand-off,

---

[36] P.A. and R.L Fanthorpe, *The Holy Grail Revealed — The Real Secret of Rennes-le-Château* (San Bernardino, Ca. 92406: Borgo Press, Second Edition, 1986), 68.

with neither party willing to lower his metaphorical gun first because his antagonist would certainly shoot if he did!

Fouquet's place as Finance Minister was taken by the sinister, scheming Colbert, another of Louis's instruments, who almost immediately sent an expedition to the Rennes-le-Château area to re-excavate and explore the original Tomb of Arques. This must have been an ancient structure once occupying the site of the relatively modern one which the authors measured and photographed in 1975. That one was built — or modified above ground level — by an American named Lawrence at the end of the nineteenth century, or during the first decade of the twentieth. It was his design which precisely emulated Poussin's final version of the legendary Arcadian Tomb. Even more curiously, Poussin's original canvas was taken to Louis's royal apartments at Versailles, before it found its way to the Louvre many years afterwards.

Bérenger Saunière was alleged to have translated and decoded some mysterious parchments which were said to have been found in the Visigothic altar pillar of the badly neglected, ancient, hilltop church of St. Mary Magdalene, which Saunière had taken over in 1885, when he was thirty-three years old. The coded message contained references to Poussin as well as to the Arcadian Treasure of Sion and the burial place of the murdered Merovingian King, Dagobert II.

"Shepherdess no temptation to which Poussin and Teniers hold the key ..." began the strange message. The shepherdess is the dominant figure in the Poussin composition. Art experts have actually analyzed the picture to show that her head is the centre of a pentagon which governs the whole design of the painting and extends outside the frame. X-rays also showed that one shepherd's staff in the foreground had been painted before the background, and the length of the staff played a critical part in the geometry of the painting.

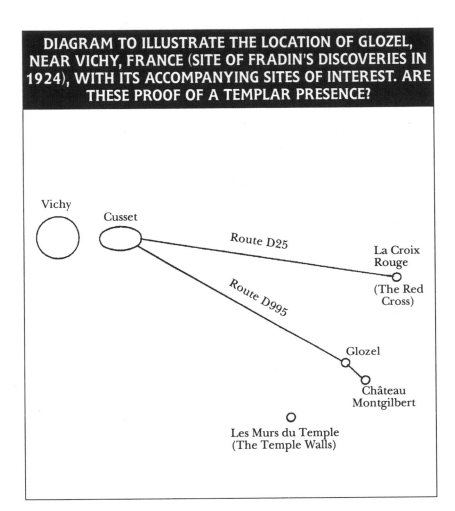

DIAGRAM TO ILLUSTRATE THE LOCATION OF GLOZEL, NEAR VICHY, FRANCE (SITE OF FRADIN'S DISCOVERIES IN 1924), WITH ITS ACCOMPANYING SITES OF INTEREST. ARE THESE PROOF OF A TEMPLAR PRESENCE?

As David Wood has pointed out with commendable care and precision in "Genisis" and "Geneset" [sic],[37] geometry is one of the major clues to the Rennes mystery, and Henry Lincoln has expounded his similar significant discoveries in *The Holy Place*.[38]

---

[37]David Wood, *Genisis*, and D. Wood and I. Campbell, *Geneset*, available via Bellevue Books, Unit E4, Sunbury International Business Centre, Brooklands Close, Sunbury on Thames, Middx. TW16 7DX, U.K.
[38]H. Lincoln, *The Holy Place* (London: Jonathan Cape Ltd., 1991).

The Tomb of Arques photographed by the authors in 1975.

Poussin's painting "The Shepherds of Arcadia," Louvre version.

But Rennes is only half of the French connection with the Arcadian Treasure and its link with Oak Island. The other half is at the tiny hamlet of Glozel near Vichy. We have spoken with Emile Fradin who actually made the discoveries in the strange pit at Glozel in 1924. We have seen the inexplicable exhibits in his Museum there. Not far to the south-east of the Fradin farm lie the imposing ruins of the thirteenth-century Château de Montgilbert — contemporary with both the Templars and the ill-fated Cathars, or Albigensians. Just a few kilometres due east of Vichy itself, and the same distance due north of Glozel and the Montgilbert Chateau, on the D7 route, is La Croix Rouge ("The Red Cross" — the symbol of the Templars). Also very close to Glozel, but lying just to the south-west of the Fradin farm, are Les Murs du Temple ("The Walls of the Temple"). Just a coincidence? Or an indication that the Templars were as closely involved with Glozel as they were with Rennes-le-Château?

What sort of pattern are all these historical threads weaving? They lead back time and again to our central hypothesis that some very ancient object — said to be a source of enormous wealth and power — was pursued across the centuries by those who knew of it, regardless of the risks involved. Did Gilgamesh and Enkidu seek it in ancient Sumeria? In the Fifth Tablet of their great Epic, they have to seek out and overcome the formidable Khumbaba, guardian of the trees. What other treasure is hidden among the sacred cedars which Khumbaba defends so desperately against the two heroic intruders?[39]

Did Abram know of it when he and his family were called by God to leave Ur of the Chaldees? What mysterious truth lay behind Sarah's legendary discovery in Hermes' cavern? Were Melchizedek, Thoth and Trismegistus three different names for the same wise and powerful man, and what secret powers lay concealed in his Emerald Tablets? Suppose, too, that the Tablets became the true core of the

---

[39]Paul Haupt, *Das babylonische Nimrodepos* (Leipzig: 1884).

mysterious Arcadian treasure, and that they went at one period from Melchizedek's Salem to Pharaoh's Egypt, only to be retrieved by Moses and eventually returned to Jerusalem in Solomon's time. Suppose that it was the reckless pursuit of those same Emerald Tablets that precipitated the pride of Pharaoh's charioteers to their deaths in the Red Sea.

Solomon dies. Some, if not all, of the Tablets find their way to Ethiopia via his son, Menelik, born to the beautiful black Queen Makeda (encoded as the lovely Belacane in Wolfram's *Parzival*). Solomon's son is accompanied by a party of his loyal Jewish supporters, who settle in Ethiopia and become the ancestors of the present-day Falashas.

Suppose that many years later there are Templars at the Ethiopian Court of Lalibela ('Prester John') in the thirteenth century, Templars at Chartres Cathedral, Templars at Château Montgilbert near Glozel, Templars at Rennes-le-Château among the carefully hidden Merovingian tombs — Templars who know about the Arcadian Treasure and the Emerald Tablets.

Then comes the tragic involvement of Philip IV, the downfall of the Middle Eastern and European Templars, the flight of the refugees to the Orkneys with part, at least, of the priceless treasure, and, finally, the Atlantic voyage.

Yet there is another complication that has to be considered very carefully before the examination of the French Connection can be satisfactorily concluded — and that complication is Sir Francis Bacon's enigmatic brother Anthony, who spent a great deal of time in France as part of the Elizabethan 'secret service.' What was Anthony so busy investigating, and what secrets did he send home to the brilliant and frequently underestimated Francis?

16

FRANCIS BACON'S
SECRET CYPHER

Francis Bacon, Baron Verulam, Viscount St. Albans, was born on January 22, 1561. (By a curious coincidence, it was on Bacon's birthday in 1917 that Bérenger Saunière died.) Francis lived until April 9, 1626, which puts him squarely inside the same time frame as Shakespeare, Spenser, Sidney, Marlowe, and the three painters who were said to 'hold the key' to the Arcadian Treasure of Rennes — Poussin and both Teniers. Bacon's other contemporaries included fellow lawyer William Anson, whose fortune founded the Shugborough Hall dynasty, and the remarkable Dr John Dee (1527–1608), wizard, astrologer, mathematician and crystal gazer. If there was a secret society of Arcadian Treasure Guardians with which the Cathars and Templars had once been closely involved, and which had later re-surfaced under the Rosicrucian banner, Dee is a very likely candidate for membership, or perhaps even control of it, in Tudor times.

Although Francis was officially accepted as the younger son of Sir Nicholas Bacon and his second wife, Ann (who was the daughter of Sir Anthony Cooke and the sister-in-law of Sir William Cecil, Lord Burghley), there are reasonable grounds for believing that he was actually the secret son of Queen Elizabeth I. One theory suggests that Francis Drake, 'the Queen's pirate,' was his natural father.

Another strong suspicion was that the father of Elizabeth's son was Lord Robert Dudley, Earl of Leicester. He had apparently arranged for the murder of his wife, Amy Robsart, at Cumnor Place, Oxfordshire, in the hope that Elizabeth would marry him. Such was the fanatical Protestant loyalty of Sir Nicholas and Lady Ann, that they would have done anything necessary to protect their beloved Queen from scandal.

Despite the possibility that he was not the biological son of Nicholas Bacon, young Francis learned a great deal from the man whom the world regarded as his father. Nicholas himself had been born circa 1510 and by dint of sheer intelligence and hard work had gained a place at Cambridge. He was in Paris for a while after leaving University and then went on to Gray's Inn to read Law. His great chance came when Archbishop Heath, who was then Lord Chancellor, declined to carry out some of Queen Elizabeth's instructions — never a prudent course to follow in Tudor times! Although not acquiring the official title of Chancellor, Sir Nicholas took over much of Heath's former work. This elder Bacon was in many ways a curious contradiction: a strangely paradoxical man. Contemporary portraits show him as grossly overweight, and give him a decidedly earthy, crafty, untrustworthy appearance — like Bumble the Beadle in Dickens' Oliver Twist.

Yet all who knew him well, and so could write of him with some accuracy and authority, commented warmly on his generosity, his kindness, his patience and understanding. Those who knew him best regarded him as a man of undoubted shrewdness, intelligence and good humour.

Historians with an interest in psychology might well wonder whether Sir Nicholas had learnt to play several roles successfully, and whether Sir Francis had subsequently acquired that trick from him. In 1564, Sir Nicholas had either written or sponsored a pamphlet which appeared under the name of John Hales, in which the royal claims of the House of Suffolk were supported. Needless to say, this was not well received by Elizabeth, and Sir Nicholas was under a cloud for some time. This experience taught him the perils of political authorship: a lesson he must have impressed firmly on young Francis after the boy's striking literary abilities became apparent.

Was Bacon the author of the plays and poems attributed to William Shakespeare (1564–1616), and possibly those attributed to Christopher Marlowe (1564–1593) as well? Undoubtedly he had more than enough talent, education and experience to have written them, and his own essays prove him capable of writing in a wide variety of styles.[40] One curious clue exists in Act five, scene one, of *Love's Labour Lost:* the polysyllabic monstrosity 'honorificabilitudinitatibus'. Baconian cryptographers have claimed that this can be re-worked into a Latin cypher meaning: 'These plays, F. Bacon's offspring, are preserved for the world'.[41] If that interpretation is correct, it lends considerable support to the theory that Bacon's original manuscripts of the works attributed to Shakespeare and Marlowe lie under their protective mercury among the other priceless treasures deep in the Oak Island labyrinth. Bacon was as much a man of science as a man of letters, and one of his theories in *Sylva Sylvarum* involved the preservation of manuscripts in mercury. Add to this the finding on Oak Island of ancient flasks with traces of mercury in them[42] and the theory becomes tenable. There is also the evidence of Mrs. Gallup's discovery of the Biliteral Cipher among Bacon's works.[43] On December 3, 1948, Dr. Burrell F. Ruth told a group of students at Iowa State College that in his opinion Bacon had hidden his original manuscripts somewhere very secure in the hope that they would one day be recovered by better citizens living in a better world.

Dr. Orville Ward Owen followed what he understood to be Baconian cyphers and found a mysterious underground

---

[40]E. Lawrence-Durning, *Bacon is Shake-Speare*, 1910, and *The Shakespeare Myth*, 1912.
[41]Paul Harvey (Ed.), *The Oxford Companion to English Literature, Fourth Edition*, revised by D.S Eagle (Oxford: Clarendon Press, 1967). 58.
[42]Darcy O'Connor, *The Big Dig* (New York: Ballantine, 1988). 218.
[43]R.L. and P.A. Fanthorpe, *Secrets of Rennes-le-Château*, (York Beach, Maine: Samuel Weiser, Inc., 1992). 101.

room beneath the bed of the River Wye in the west of Britain. It was empty, but Dr. Owen found further Baconian cyphers cut into its walls. In Owen's opinion, Bacon had originally intended to conceal his priceless manuscripts below the Wye, in much the same way that the ancient Visigoths had dammed and diverted rivers, constructed burial chambers beneath them, and then allowed the waters to flow back over the last resting place of their dead leader and his treasure. This was certainly done for Alaric, the Visigothic conqueror of Rome. Owen concluded that Bacon had had second thoughts and had decided that the chamber near the mouth of the Wye was not secure enough. Had he then chosen a much safer hiding place farther afield? In 1610, King James I granted Bacon land in Newfoundland, giving him a close connection with the early history of Canada.

Francis and his elder brother Anthony had attended Cambridge University together in 1573 and studied under that same Dr. Whitgift, who became Archbishop of Canterbury. As a young man in 1576, Bacon was in France with the Ambassador, Sir Amias Paulet, and remained there until 1579. It may have been Paulet (or some other English aristocrat who was party to the secret) who during this time informed Francis of his 'real' parentage. Anthony spent a much longer period in Europe, not returning to England until 1591.

Both the brothers had met influential Huguenots during their time abroad, and the Huguenots were reputed to have had links with the Cathars.

How does all of this connect Bacon with the Arcadian Treasure, the Emerald Tablets and the Oak Island Money Pit? Firstly, Bacon's legal background links him with Anson of Shugborough and the Shepherd Monument, which in turn is connected with Poussin who was a contemporary of Bacon's, as Anson was.

Secondly, Bacon was in the ascendant in 1613, having just been appointed attorney general. In 1614 the key document of Rosicrucianism, *Fama Fraternatis*, appeared.

According to this strange book, Christian Rosencreutz had been buried in 1484 in a mysterious hidden tomb engraved with the words: "I shall open after 120 years". The authors of *Fama Fraternatis* claimed that they had found this heptagonal crypt in 1604 (after the expiry of Rosencreutz's 120 years — and the same year in which Bacon was appointed King's Counsel) and that it was lit by some inexplicable source. They also claimed to have examined Rosencreutz's perfectly preserved body beneath an altar surrounded by magic mirrors.[44] They said they had seen an arcane manuscript simply referred to as *The Book T,* one possible implication being that the 'T' stood for Thoth (alias Melchizedek, or Hermes Trismegistus). If there was an ancient secret Order which had been guarding the Arcadian Treasure since its earliest days, then some influential members of that Order may well have worn Cathar robes, Templar armour, and later Rosicrucian and Masonic insignia.

Francis Bacon was well known for his interest in codes and cyphers, as well as in ancient mysteries and allegories. In his preface to *The Wisdom of the Ancients* he wrote: " ... under some of the ancient fictions lay couched certain mysteries ... even from their first invention ..."[45] It was his friend, Ben Jonson, who wrote of Bacon on his sixtieth birthday:

> Hail! happy genius of this ancient Pile!
> How comes it all things so about thee smile?
> The fire! the wine! the men! and in the midst
> Thou standst as if some mystery thou didst ...
> (January 22nd, 1621)

It was also Ben Jonson who said of him: "... he seemed to me ... one of the greatest men ... that had been in many ages ..."[46]

Thirdly, if Bacon was the author of some of the great plays and poems attributed to Marlowe and Shakespeare

---

[44]George MacDonald, *Lilith,* Lion Paperback Edition, 1982 reprint of 1895 original, p. 11, reference to a magic mirror acting as a window into a strange, faërie realm.
[45]Francis Bacon, *The Essays* (Long Acre, London: Odhams Press Ltd.), 204.
[46]Ben Jonson, "Discoveries, made upon men and matter," 1641.

— perhaps even a few of the works which were attributed to Edmund Spenser (1552–99) and Sir Philip Sidney (1554–86) as well — then he would have had a powerful motive for announcing his authorship to posterity. Spenser and Sidney were good friends: Spenser, in fact, never ceased to grieve over Sidney's early death as the result of a wound inflicted in battle. Spenser's most famous work *The Faerie Queene* was intended to run to twelve books, but only six were completed.[47] The first book is concerned with the adventures of the Red Cross Knight of Holiness, regarded by most critics as an emblem of the Anglican Church, but which might equally well have stood for the Templars, whose symbol was undeniably a red cross. If Spenser is linked to the Templars, Sidney is linked to Arcadia. He is also linked to Sir William Cecil, Lord Burghley, brother-in-law to Ann Bacon, wife of Nicholas, and, ostensibly, mother of Francis. Sidney travelled a great deal. He knew France and Austria well. Although he died before Poussin was born, Sidney knew Tintoretto and Paolo Veronese, the great painters, whom he met in Venice. There was a strong cohesion and continuity among artists of that era, amounting almost to a guild or fraternity, in which secrets could easily be passed from one generation of painters to the next.

Tintoretto and Paolo may well have known something of what Poussin was later to communicate to Fouquet and to conceal in his Arcadian Shepherd canvases, with subjects' hands formed into Ogham letters. It was to Sir Philip Sidney that Spenser dedicated his famous *Shepheards Calender,* and Sidney himself wrote *Arcadia,* a series of romantic adventures set in the idyllic land of the same name. Knowing his death was imminent, Sidney tried to recall all copies of this work: why? Did it contain some clue

---

[47]Even this twelve-book scheme for the *Faerie Queene* constitutes only half of Spenser's proposed work. As Spenser himself explained in an open letter to Sir Walter Raleigh, "I labour to pourtraict in Arthure, before he was king, the image of a braue knight, perfected in the twelue priuate morall vertues, as Aristotle hath deuised, the which is the purpose of these first twelue bookes: which if I finde to be well accepted, I may be perhaps encoraged, to frame the other part of polliticke vertues in his person, after that hee came to be king." — *The Poetical Works of Edmund Spenser*, Smith & Selincourt (eds.), (Oxford: Oxford University Press), 407.

to the Arcadian Treasure, which the dying adventurer felt pointed rather too clearly to its true nature and whereabouts?

Fourthly, Bacon had special scientific knowledge of document preservation, together with an interest in Canadian land.

Fifthly, there is the scrap of parchment brought up on the drill which penetrated one of the 'treasure vaults' below the Money Pit, the scrap of paper which Doctor Porter examined so carefully and so publicly. Was that tiny fragment bearing the letters 'ui' or 'vi' torn from one of Bacon's original manuscripts?

The most fascinating data, however, are the Baconian Watermark Codes, which Mrs. Henry Pott researched with great persistence and thoroughness prior to the publication of her uniquely informative book in 1891. (The authors are fortunate in possessing the actual signed copy which Mrs.Pott gave to Lord Beauchamp in February, 1892.)

Mrs. Pott produced a mass of detailed evidence from which she concluded that Bacon had been a prominent member of a very knowledgeable secret society (Masons? Rosicrucians? Vestigial successors to the Templars?) and that that society was still active and powerful in her own day. The intriguing watermark codes which she collected and reproduced included:

1. Watermark showing elongated grapes from Sir Philip Sidney's *Arcadia,* edition dated 1662.

2. Watermark showing circular grapes surmounted by a diamond, or a dagger blade, also from Sir Philip Sidney's *Arcadia,* edition dated 1662.

3. Watermark showing rounded grapes with curious leaf, or figure emerging from water, above them, taken from the 1638 edition of Sir Francis Bacon's *Sylva Sylvarum* (the book which contains the details of storing documents in mercury to preserve them).

4. Watermark from the same source as 3 above, showing a diamond pattern of circular grapes surmounted by a hook, or crescent.

5. This is a particularly interesting pattern, resembling a stylised picture of a tree in a tub ready to be replanted (as per Michael Bradley's fascinating theory that trees were deliberately planted on Oak Island to identify it for later parties of trans-Atlantic refugees). It is from the 1669 edition of Sir Francis Bacon's *The New Atlantis*.

6. Watermark from a letter dated 1580 from H. Maynard to Anthony Bacon, now in the Tennison MSS collection, showing a tall wine-jug with an ornate lid surmounted by five crosses supporting a crown. Do these Templar symbols indicate the Order's support of Baldwin, King of Jerusalem? Or its support for 'Prester John' alias Lalibela of Ethiopia?

7. & 8. Similar wine-jug watermarks from the same source as 6, but their details differ markedly.

9. Another wine-jug watermark, of distinct pattern, found on a letter from Sir Francis Bacon to W. Doylie, dated 1580, Tennison MSS.

10. Wine jug watermark surmounted by Fleur-de-Lys emblem found on a letter from Sir Amyas Powlett [sic] to Anthony Bacon, dated 1580, Cotton MSS.

BACONIAN WATERMARKS

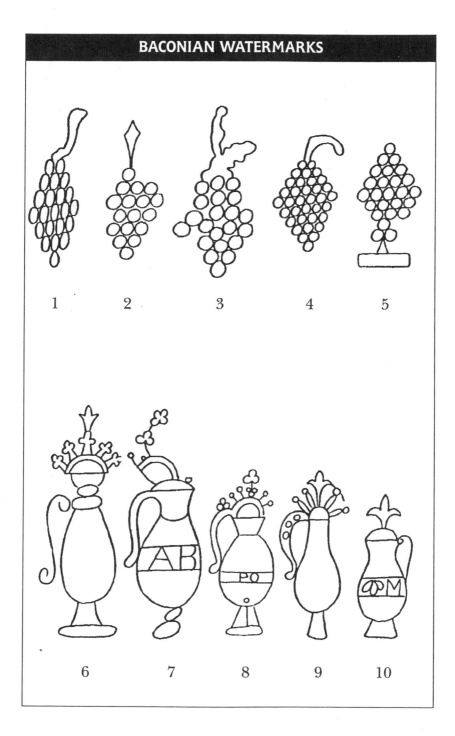

Cathars, Templars, Rosicrucians and the Tudor men of mystery like Francis and Anthony Bacon have created riddles enough: yet there is still much more to be said about the Oak Island enigma. Bacon may quite possibly have arranged for the burial of his priceless manuscripts in a preservative mercury bath somewhere in the labyrinth below the Money Pit, but, if he did, in locating Oak Island at all he was probably making use of much older, stranger knowledge and ancient arcane secrets that had been handed down to him.

17

SOMETHING OLDER
AND STRANGER

When Smith, Vaughan and McGinnis re-opened the mystery of the Money Pit in 1795, the general theory among their friends and acquaintances in the Chester and Mahone Bay area was that pirates — and most probably William Kidd's men — were responsible. Hadn't mysterious lights been seen on that sinister island a few years previously, and hadn't the men who had rowed out to investigate never returned? Wasn't that a strong enough indication that they'd been murdered by pirates who'd wanted to guard the secret of their treasure?

The Onslow Company's work in 1803 and 1804 cast the first shadowy finger of doubt over the simple pirates' buried treasure theory. What did all these layers of oak logs, of putty, of coconut fibre and of charcoal really signify? Was this the way that lazy, brutal, alcoholic, and notoriously undisciplined buccaneers normally did things? Wasn't a ten-foot hole in the sand a few yards above high watermark more their style? Measure so many paces from a rock landmark and an unusual tree? Scrawl a few compass bearings and the latitude and longitude on a crudely inaccurate sketch-map?

Doubt was also cast on the pirate theory by the discovery of the lettered stone which no one could decipher: that very unusual slab of smooth, flat, red-tinted Egyptian porphyry. What was it doing ninety feet down a pirates' hole off the coast of Nova Scotia? There was also the problem of the insuperable water: if the pit was liable to flood at that depth, how had the pirates succeeded in digging it and burying their treasure there in the first place?

By the time that the Truro Company made their attempts in the mid-nineteenth century, Jotham B. McCully's findings via the pod-auger, and Pitblado's theft of what might have been a gemstone (or something stranger and more valuable?), serious doubts were pushing the pirates' treasure theory towards the sidelines. The discovery of the long and elaborate flood tunnels, the drainage network on the beach and the treasure chamber (or burial chamber?) drastically reduced the likelihood that traditional pirates, or privateers, were responsible. What a well-equipped and well-organised labour force could not retrieve must have been concealed and defended by an even larger and better organised construction team. Who then? British Army Engineers at the time of the War of Independence? Spanish Conquistadores, or Inca refugees trying to escape from them? Drake's hardy Devonshire lads augmented by expert Cornish tin-miners? Or was it Glooscap-Sinclair with the Zeno brothers and their Templar refugees?

Go back earlier still: were they Viking sea-warriors, Romano-Celts from the old Welsh Ogofau goldmine, or George Young's Coptic refugees from Egypt?

Consider the mystery of the massive ancient timbers, submerged below Smith's Cove, still bearing their challenging Roman numerals. Part of a sixteenth century Basque fishing station? One of their ship repair yards? An early whaling or cod-salting depot? Or the remains of something as old as the proud Empire whose distinctive numerals the ancient timbers carry?

The deeper the mystery is plumbed, the stranger the discoveries which are made: there is the further riddle of the inexplicable Cave-in Pit; the labyrinth below Borehole-10X; the boxes of 'loose metal' that Fred Blair drilled into in 1897; the amazing television pictures that Blankenship's team studied; the strategically placed drilled boulders and the stone triangle pointing to something of great importance.

When a mystery is as complex as this, the solution must match it in complexity.

There is no swift, simple solution to the mystery of the Oak Island Money Pit because the phenomena being investigated do not have one simple, isolated cause.

In the oldest of the buildings in the mysterious French village of Rennes-les-Bains, Roman stonework overlays Celtic foundations, Visigothic walls hide Roman architecture, Merovingian houses have replaced Visigothic cottages and medieval masons have modified the work of their Merovingian predecessors. Archaeologists can find traces of layer upon layer of occupation and alteration there. So it is with Oak Island. The facts appear to contradict one another simply because there is so much overlapping data. Exactly the same problem arose at Glozel. What appeared to be very ancient remains — things from Palaeolithic or Mesolithic times — were found alongside artifacts from the first century of the Christian era, and other pieces from the thirteenth and fourteenth centuries AD. It didn't make sense said the tradition-bound French archaeologists of the 'twenties. They dismissed it all as a hoax. Thermo-luminescent dating in Scottish and Scandinavian Universities in the 1970s, however, proved conclusively that the artifacts at Glozel were genuinely old: there was no possible way that they could have been faked by the Fradin family in 1924. The apparent contradiction was absolute: a compromise theory had to be found.

What if the so-called medieval 'glass factory' at Glozel had also been the lair of a 'witch' or 'wizard'? Someone who had collected the ancient artifacts because he, or she, believed that they possessed 'magical' qualities? That would have accounted both for the archaeological incompatibility of the excavated objects, and for their genuine antiquity.

Where and when did the Oak Island Money Pit mystery

really begin? What forms the first detectable layer of this intricately laminated puzzle?

It began a long way from Nova Scotia, and a long time before 1795. The legends of the ancient, anthropomorphic 'gods' and 'goddesses' (beings credited with great longevity and superior powers to those of normal humanity) must have had some foundation other than wishful thinking and a strong desire to emulate their advantages. Just as palaeontology and anthropology record the differences between *Ramapithecus, Australopithecus, Homo habilis* of the Olduvai Gorge, Heidelberg, Peking, Cro-Magnon and Neanderthal humanity, so there may well have existed other species and sub-species, families and genuses differing as much from us as from one another, or from the Yeti and the Sasquatch. What was J.R.R. Tolkien really hinting at when he situated his super-human Númenoreans in a western kingdom known as Atalantë in the Quenya language?[48]

The very knowledgeable C.S. Lewis (a close friend of Tolkien) hinted in *That Hideous Strength* that Merlin the Magician, famed in the Arthurian legends, was one of the last survivors of this ancient and immensely powerful Númenorean race.[49]

Von Däniken, by contrast, would argue that such beings came originally from a strange, faraway planet. Atlantis, Lemuria or the Belt of Orion — whether they eventually turn out to be terrestrial humanity's closest, or most distant, cousins — their origin is shrouded in prehistoric myth and mystery. One name stands out boldly from that vast ancient plurality of gods and goddesses, nature spirits and demons, djinns and elementals, demi-gods and magicians: that name is Thoth, teacher and scribe of the Egyptian gods; Thoth who is otherwise known as Hermes Trismegistus, and very probably as Melchizedek; Thoth who is always on the side of light, of wisdom, of truth and

---

[48]Robert Foster, *The Complete Guide to Middle-Earth* (New York: Ballantine Books, 1978), 384.
[49]C.S. Lewis, *That Hideous Strength* (London: Pan Books Paperback Edition, 1980), 172.

of goodness. It is Thoth, the great lore-master, who dares to challenge and thwart the dark designs of Set, the sinister, evil entity of Egyptian mythology.

The power and wisdom of Thoth are said to reside in his mysterious Emerald Tablets. Exactly what those Tablets are, or what they are able to achieve, only a very few of the most avant-garde thinkers would dare to speculate: but they are said to be truly awesome, ranking alongside the energy which generated the controversial Philadelphia Experiment and allegedly blew the *Eldridge* through hyperspace in 1943.[50] Their power may also be compared with the energy involved in the alarming Montauk Project on Long Island, New York.[51] It has been conjectured that there is a power within the Emerald Tablets capable of warping Time and Space themselves, of opening the science fiction writers' so-called 'gates' between 'probability tracks' and 'parallel universes,' of determining which probability track shall cease to be hypothetical and become a concrete, experiential 'reality.'

In summary then, Hermes Trismegistus (alias Thoth, alias Melchizedek?) clearly stands in the front rank of those ancient beings whose origin is unknown but who were apparently capable of exercising vast and mysterious powers not available to their normal, human contemporaries. When Abram returned from the Jordanian war during which he rescued his kinsman, Lot, he encountered Melchizedek, priest-king of Salem, and gave him a tenth of the spoils captured in the war. Psalm 76 verse 2 equates Salem with Sion and Jerusalem. Psalm 110 — usually regarded as a Messianic Psalm — refers to Melchizedek's endless life. In the New Testament Letter to the Hebrews, chapter 7, the writer describes Melchizedek as being "... without father, without mother, without descent, having neither beginning of days nor end of life, but made like

---

[50]C. Berlitz, and W. Moore, *The Philadelphia Experiment* (London: Souvenir Press, 1979, Granada Paperbacks, 1980). B. Steiger, A. Beilek, and S. Hanson-Steiger, *The Philadelphia Experiment and Other UFO Conspiracies* (New Brunswick, New Jersey, Box 753, 08903: Timewalker Productions, Inner Light Publications, 1990).

[51]P.B. Nichols and P .Moon, *The Montauk Project* (Westbury, New York, Box 769, 11590: Sky Books, 1992).

unto the Son of God ..."

Ancient Egyptian legend and mythology, augmented by later Greek scholarship at Alexandria, credited Thoth (Melchizedek?) with the authorship of many books of wisdom dealing with such diverse fields of knowledge as astronomy, astrology, mathematics, history, geography and medicine. He is also said to have been the author of the *Book of the Dead*, whose earliest versions go back at least as far as 4000 BC[52]

Two assumptions may now reasonably be made: that a very wise, powerful and mysterious being known variously in ancient times as Thoth, Hermes Trismegistus and Melchizedek was a genuine historical character, and that this same being was the possessor of certain devices, often described as the Emerald Tablets, by the use of which some of his enormous super-human powers were exercised.

It is equally safe to assume that those who coveted such powers would have gone to any lengths to acquire the Emerald Tablets, and that he who possessed them would have taken great care to ensure that they never fell into the wrong hands — especially into the hands of those who followed Set, the personification of evil in ancient Egypt.

Here then, millennia before the Christian era, is the earliest and faintest dawning of the Arcadian Treasure quest. Rennes-le-Château has its dark and terrible secrets right enough, but they are not even remotely connected with Jesus, with Mary Magdalene, with the totally imaginary 'bloodline' hypothesised by Baigent, Lincoln and Leigh,[53] with Joseph of Arimathea, or with the Holy Grail as the Sacred Vessel from which Christ shared wine with His disciples at the Last Supper. That priceless Sacred Vessel may well have been miraculously preserved somewhere, but its quest and its saga are a totally different story. They follow a different route entirely from the trail of

---

[52]L. Spence, *Myths and Legends of Ancient Egypt* (London: George G. Harrap and Co., Dover 1990 reprint), 106–107.
[53]M. Baigent, R.Leigh, and H. Lincoln, *The Holy Blood and the Holy Grail* (London: Corgi Edition, 1983).

the Emerald Tablets at the heart of the Arcadian Treasure.

That the far, far older Grailstone tradition may have been given a Christian veneer by early evangelists and missionaries (as many other ancient pagan festivals and mysteries were given) is highly likely. That the medieval knightly romance of the quest for the Holy Grail, in the form of Christ's Cup, may have become confused in the telling with the hunt for the Grailstone, Grail Tablet or Hermetic Crystals is also highly likely, and would account for much of the confusion surrounding the Grail saga today. The theory that the 'secret' of Rennes-le-Château has anything to do with some sensational 'revelation' contradicting the crucifixion and resurrection of Christ is totally false. The Christ revealed to us in the Gospels and the Apostles' Creed is a physical, historical and spiritual fact. The real Arcadian Treasure mystery which links Rennes, Glozel and Oak Island presents no challenge at all to the great central truths of Christianity.

As Wolfram makes plain in his apparently deeply coded epic, *Parzival,* the Grail of antiquity was a stone of some sort, a crystal, perhaps, or a gemstone tablet, rather than a drinking vessel.

In their earliest days the Emerald Tablets moved from ancient Egypt to Salem and back again more than once: it was as if some great psychic tug-of-war was going on between Hermes Trismegistus and Set. Perhaps word of them reached Ur of the Chaldees at about the time that Abram began his long journeyings. Was there a vestige of truth in the ancient Jewish legend that Sarah, Abram's sister-wife, came across them by accident in the cavern where Hermes rested (in much the same way that Christian Rosencreutz later rested in his heptagonal tomb)? Perhaps it was when the Emerald Tablets left Egypt with Moses that an evil Pharaoh (a follower of Set?) hurled his doomed charioteers in suicidal pursuit of them across the bed of the Red Sea.

Did the Tablets next find centuries of safety inside the Ark of the Covenant in the Holy of Holies — a place so vibrant with sacred power that Set's agents dared not approach it directly? What happened shortly before Solomon died? Did Menelik, Son of the Wise Man, succeed in taking the Ark to his beautiful mother's distant Kingdom of Ethiopia, and, if so, did he gain possession of all the Emerald Tablets, or only some of them? What do the Ethiopian Holy Men guard so zealously at Axum today? The empty Ark?

A thin line of ancient Gnostic tradition links unusual early religious groups such as the Paulicians, the Manicheans, the Bogomils and the Cathars: far more discernible bonds connect the Cathars to the Templars and the Templars to modern Freemasonry. Suppose that Gnosticism, which had a dualistic view of the universe, and which percolated strongly through the Cathar beliefs, also guarded some of the secret knowledge of the Arcadian Treasure and the Emerald Tablets which formed its priceless and powerful core. Gnostic dualism would readily embrace the concept of a holy war between Hermes Trismegistus, representing Goodness and Light, and Set, representing Evil and Darkness. The very early Coptic fragment in the British Museum, the *Pistis Sophia,* is a piece of Gnostic teaching. George Young believes (with sound logic to back him) that Coptic refugees found their way to Oak Island. The riddle carved into the ancient red porphyry slab in the Money Pit may also have been inscribed in some variant Coptic dialect if Professor Barry Fell is correct.

But another possible refuge for all or some of the Emerald Tablets and the Arcadian Treasure has yet to be considered. North-Eastern Spain and South-western France (the area including Rennes-le-Château and Rennes-les-Bains) were once the largely independent Jewish Principality of Septimania.

Baigent, Lincoln and Leigh have obscured the issue somewhat in their enthusiasm to find evidence for their incorrect 'Bloodline of Jesus and Mary Magdalene' theory, but a significant portion of their ancillary historical research remains sound. As they themselves point out, there was a semi-autonomous Jewish Principality in the Rennes area which flourished during the sixth and seventh centuries AD. One of its most notably successful rulers was Guillem de Gallone who was the hero of another of Wolfram's epic tales, and who was also traditionally associated with the Guardians of the Grail. What if Guillem was actually another of the secret guardians of the Emerald Tablets? Where did his Septimanian Jews come from originally? Did they, by any chance, leave at the same time that Menelik and his companions brought the Ark of the Covenant to Axum?[54]

The threads now begin to come together again, and a clearer pattern starts to emerge. Among the most mysterious objects referred to in the Bible are the Urim and Thummim. They are first mentioned in Exod. 28:30 as being placed in the jewelled Breastplate of Judgment worn by the High Priest — indeed, the text implies that this is the purpose of the Breastplate. While the instructions for making the Breastplate are given in considerable detail (verses 15 to 29), neither here nor anywhere else in the Scriptures are any instructions for making the Urim and Thummim, or even one word about what they looked like or how they were used.

The Urim and Thummim might have been jewels; they might have been sacred engraved stones; they might have been auxiliary components of the main Emerald Tablets. They were once used to ascertain the Will of Yahweh, rather as lots were cast to make important decisions, or to resolve vital questions. They gave guiding 'signs' in much the same way that Gideon, the courageous Judge of Israel, asked Yahweh for a 'sign' via the fleece and the morning dew.[55]

Somewhere along the winding road of Hebrew history, the Urim and Thummim vanished. There were no more

---

[54]M. Baigent, R. Leigh, and H. Lincoln, *The Holy Blood and the Holy Grail* (London: Corgi Paperback Edition, 1983), 412.
[55]Judg. 6:37, et seq.

priests who knew how to read them. Could they have left the Holy Land at the same time as the Ark made its way to Axum? Did they travel with those same Jews who brought the Ark to Solomon's son, King Menelik of Ethiopia? Did they later find their way to Septimania during its prosperity? Were they concealed there for safety (along with other precious Jewish and Arcadian Treasures at Rennes-le-Château) when the glory of Septimania began to fade?

From Rennes to Glozel near Vichy is barely 200 miles as the crow flies — no problem for an experienced and determined horseman, and even less for a party of dedicated, veteran Templar Knights, armed to the teeth and ready for anything. If the grim disciples of Set were in pursuit of that powerful and priceless treasure — which must never be allowed to fall into their sinister hands — would not the wisest course have been to separate its various components, and place them in different, secret locations: Rennes, Glozel — and, eventually, somewhere far away across the wide and formidable Atlantic? Modern firearm safety regulations recommend permit holders to keep ammunition locked in one police-approved safe, and unloaded guns in another. Would not a parallel thought have occurred to the wise old guardians of the Arcadian Treasure? With Glooscap/Sinclair support, part of it, at least, could have made its way across the Atlantic to the deep safety of the strange Oak Island labyrinth, the earliest parts of which already waited below Oak Island.

Here, then, is the innermost heart of the great secret: the final and breath-taking truth about the Money Pit and all that lies below it, and alongside it. There are no simple answers which automatically exclude all others, because the whole structure is ancient and composite. It is a laminated arcane honeycomb, a convoluted catacomb of secrets, riddles and enigmas. Daedalus himself would have been proud to have created such a structure. The Gordian Knot is a mere clove-hitch beside this vast Oak Island Mystery.

Phoenician and Carthaginian traders were among the first to reach Mahone Bay; fourth century Romano-Celtic

Legionaries and miners from Ogofau dug and delved below what is now the Money Pit; Coptic refugees survived the perilous Atlantic voyage and left their Egyptian porphyry memorial stone behind them with the revered body of their leader, the *Arif*. Perhaps many years were to elapse before later visitors accidentally disturbed it, recognized it for something sacred and mysterious, and reverently re-interred it in their own comparatively recent shaft.

Photograph of the top of the Money Pit.

Sinclair's Templars arrived with their precious cargo and more work was carried out: vast, natural, limestone caverns and twisting subterranean passages were augmented by additional connecting ways, flood traps and water barriers to guard the priceless Emerald Tablets which the Templars had brought with them. Then, perhaps, Drake's Cornish miners added a passageway and chamber or two to what was already there — for readily understandable buccaneering reasons. Suppose that the historical sensation to cap all historical sensations is valid: Francis Bacon really was Drake's illegitimate son by Queen Elizabeth! If

Drake himself already knew about the Oak Island mystery, wouldn't that have been the link which would have enabled his son, Sir Francis Bacon, to preserve important documents there, using the new mercury-bath method which he had pioneered?

Henry Morgan had the charisma and the organising ability to make his own distinctive contribution to the complexity that already existed below the island. So did King George III's *clique,* which included the fabulously wealthy Admiral Anson of Shugborough Hall. Perhaps from Anson — or from one of his trusted navigational officers — there came a faint, indiscreet whisper that George III's Havana gold was hidden below the island, and that a marvellous, impregnable hiding place already existed there. If that rumour reached an English Engineering Officer during the American War of Independence, it might well have prompted him to bury the army pay-chests there: and later retrieve them!

There is no single treasure, there are several ... and most important of all are the Emerald Tablets. There was no single Unknown Genius, there were several, and each added something significant to the work of his predecessors. Those who dug and concealed over so many centuries have that much in common with those who have sought, and are still seeking: as with all human endeavour, the work of those who follow, depends upon the foundations laid by those who went before them. It is fitting, perhaps, to end with a tribute to the three 1795 pioneers: a picture of all that is left of the foundations of one of the homesteads they built on the island when they combined farming with treasure-hunting so long ago.

Photograph of the foundations of the McGinnis home or that of another early settler on Oak Island.

Appendix 1

Terry Ross Investigates

While staying with Dr.Bob, Zohara and Anna Hieronimus, and their friend Laura Cortner, in Owings Mills, near Baltimore, Maryland, in November, 1993, we received many great kindnesses. Not least of these was an introduction to the celebrated and gifted psychic, T.E. Ross. He shares our interest in Rennes-le-Château and in the Oak Island Money Pit mystery, and gave us his reactions — both as an expert in paranormal phenomena, and a gifted psychic in his own right — to various aspects of those enigmas.

We asked him first about the mainland camp which the original Money Pit builders were supposed to have established, and which George Young had shown us as a result of its being identified by a psychic friend of his. Terry Ross confirmed what George had said, and added that this camp site would be worth investigating.

When asked for his psychic response to the Stone Triangle he felt that it was of genuine importance, but that it pointed to a significant clue rather than to the heart of the mystery itself. In response to our questions about the inscribed porphyry slab found at around the ninety-foot level in 1803/4, he said it had a strange feeling, and that it was nothing to do with pirates, except perhaps later in a superficial way. Terry felt that the stone was involved with the centre of the mystery, with the centre of all the expeditions which had set out and put up the standing stone structures in New England and everywhere else. He said he thought it was probably connected with activities which took place around 2000 BC.

Terry also felt strongly that the people responsible for it had a Mediterranean connection. His comments on what he referred to as their 'mindset' were very interesting indeed. "The mindset of these people seems utterly and totally different from anything we know today. They were friends of the earth and their whole motivation and energy were being expended to nurture the earth and be nurtured by her."

He then went on to talk about some fascinating archaeological work in Ohio in which he had been involved. "The mounds we've investigated in Ohio had seven levels — like Silbury Hill, in Wiltshire, England. The archaeologists sliced one mound all the way down . . . We found independently that there were seven layers of earth in it — like a battery, you know. One of the layers came from Iowa — all the way from Iowa to Ohio. They don't know of anywhere else where that earth is found. That would account for some very strange stones turning up in important places. The Oak Island Money Pit stone was probably brought with the people who came from the Mediterranean. It has a centring effect for whatever they wanted to do there."

Terry gets the feeling that the flood tunnels were definitely a protective device.

When asked about Pitblado and his role in the Oak Island mystery, Terry had strong 'negative vibes'. "He's not a very savoury man; that's the first feeling I have. I think that what he found was not, perhaps, all that critical or important, but he thought it was. I don't think it contained a secret or the clue to any riches. In fact I have an awful time finding riches in connection with this whole thing."

We then asked him whether we (and all the other investigators!) had been looking at the Money Pit in entirely the wrong way. Were all its elaborate precautions and defences designed to keep something very dangerous in, rather than to keep intruders out? Terry said that he thought whoever had built it had had an entirely different motivation from that of contemporary humanity. He felt that a different approach to the problem was needed. When we asked him how different, how alien, the originators were, he replied that he got a strange sensation about them — laughingly he used the word 'spooky.' He had the distinct feeling that there was a connection with something very unusual, a feeling that there was 'a back and forth of information and instructions'. The Money Pit, perhaps contained some kind of 'implant' that was necessary for future developments. "I think that this is connected with earth changes to be . . . It's that drastic in my mind. These people, super-engineers that they were, were the only ones that could have pulled this off in that whole range of time. They were prevailed upon to do so."

When asked about Rennes-le-Château, the Scottish Sinclair-Templar connection and Mike Bradley's "Two Oak Islands" theory, Terry felt that they were all involved to a greater or lesser extent. He felt that this was a mystery that "went right back through the Corridors of Time ... almost to the Garden of Eden".

In response to our final question about Fred Nolan and his recent discovery with William S. Crooker of the supposed huge Templar Cross on Oak Island, Terry said, "Nolan's a decent fellow, and he's holding on to some ideas that don't fit in with the others." Just as Pitblado had produced a negative psychic response, so our mention of Nolan's work produced a strongly positive one.

Appendix 2

George Young, Glozel and the Yarmouth Stone

George Young, who unlocked the amazing connection between the Ogham hand-sign alphabet and Poussin's strangely coded Arcadian paintings, has made another very significant discovery. The authors gave George detailed information about the mysterious and highly controversial Glozel alphabet, which they themselves studied on site in the early 1970s. George related this to his own special knowledge of Ogham and the curious Yarmouth Stone, now carefully preserved in the Yarmouth County Museum, Nova Scotia.

This 400-pound boulder, which was discovered in a salt-marsh by a Yarmouth family doctor, Richard Fletcher, in 1812, bears an inscription consisting of only fourteen characters. Numerous experts have puzzled over it for nearly two centuries. Olaf Strandwold, an eminent Norwegian scholar, believes that the characters are runic, and that they can be translated to mean "Leif to Eric raises [this monument] ..." The idea of "this monument" following "raises" is understood, rather than actually inscribed on the stone. Leif Ericsson and his father, and their adventurous voyages are referred to in detail in Chapter 12, "Celts and Vikings", on page 135.

Other scholars believe that the inscription is the work of Micmac Indians, or that the characters are Japanese. Another school of thought credits early Basque fishermen with the work, and translates the inscription to read "The Basque people have conquered this land."

It is only when Dr. Morlet's extensive studies of Glozel and its weird alphabet[1] are combined with George Young's keen perception that the most likely explanation of the Yarmouth Stone's inscription is forthcoming. Far from detracting from the Stone's historical interest and importance, a connection with the Glozel Alphabet — which appears to be much older than the Viking Runes — greatly enhances the Stone's importance and raises a score of intriguing questions about how long it lay in Dr. Fletcher's saltmarsh, who inscribed it, and how they reached Nova Scotia.

Here are the characters inscribed on the Yarmouth Stone, set alongside their Glozel counterparts, numbered according to Dr. Morlet's categorisation on pages 31 and 32 of his *Origines de l'Ecriture*.[1]

Yarmouth Stone														

| | | | | or | | | | | | | | | | |

| Glozel Alphabet | | | | | | | | | | | | | | |

| Morlet's Numbering | 4 | 16 | 15 | 31 or 44 | 24 | 65 | 41 | 32 | 15 | 16 | 14 | 24 | 43 | 1 |

[1]A. Morlet, *Origines de l'Ecriture* (7 Rue Dom-Vaissette, Montpelier, France: Cause, Graille & Castelnau, 1955).

Bibliography

Armstrong, Richard, et al. *Treasure and Treasure Hunters*. London: Hamish Hamilton, 1969.

Bacon, F. *The Wisdom of the Ancients and The New Atlantis*. London: Odhams, (undated).

Baigent, M., Leigh, R. and Lincoln, H. *The Holy Blood and the Holy Grail*. London: Corgi, 1983.

Baigent, M., Leigh, R. and Lincoln, H. *The Messianic Legacy*. London: Corgi, 1987.

Baigent, M. and Leigh, R. *The Temple and the Lodge*. London: Corgi, 1990.

Berlitz, C. and Moore, W. *The Philadelphia Experiment*. London: Souvenir Press, 1979.

Birks, W. and Gilbert, R. A. *The Treasure of Montségur*. London: Aquarian Press, 1987.

Bonfanti, L. *Biographies and Legends of the New England Indians*. Wakefield, Mass.: Pride Publications, 1981.

Botting, D. *The Pirates*. Amsterdam: Time-Life Books.

Boudet, Henri. *La Vraie Langue Celtique et le Cromleck de Rennes-les-Bains*. Nice, France: Belisane, 1984 reprint.

Bradley, M. and Theilmann-Bean, D. *Holy Grail Across the Atlantic*. Toronto: Hounslow Press, 1988.

Bradford, E. *Drake*. London: Hodder and Stoughton, 1967.

Brookesmith, P. *Open Files Volume 6*. containing 'The Enigma of Oak Island', London: Orbis Publishing, 1984.

Captier, A. and M. and Marrot, M. *Rennes-le-Château: le Secret de l'Abbé Saunière*. Nice, France: Belisane, 1985.

Carpenter, H. *The Inklings: C. S. Lewis, J. R. R. Tolkien, Charles Williams and Their Friends*. London: George Allen and Unwin, 1978.

Carpenter, H. *The Letters of J. R. R. Tolkien*. Boston: Houghton Mifflin, 1981.

Cavendish, R. *Encyclopedia of the Unexplained*. London: Routledge and Kegan Paul, 1974.

Chetwynd, T. *Dictionary of Sacred Myth*. London: Aquarian Press, 1986.

Clark, A. H. *Acadia: The Geography of Early Nova Scotia to 1760*. Madison, Wisconsin: University of Wisconsin Press, 1968.

Cochran, E. B. N. (Editor and President). *The Nova Scotia Historical Society Papers 1878–1884*. Belleville, Ontario: Mika Publishing Co., 1976.

Cotterell, A. *A Dictionary of World Mythology*. Oxford: Oxford University Press, 1986.

Crane, P. *Miracles and Modern Science*. Sussex, UK: Crane Publications, 1991.

Crooker, William S. *The Oak Island Quest*. Windsor, Nova Scotia: Lancelot Press, 1978.

Crooker, William S. *Oak Island Gold*. Halifax, Nova Scotia: Nimbus Publishing Ltd., 1993.

de Sede, Gerard, *Rennes-le-Château: les enigmes de l'univers*. Paris: Robert Laffont, 1988.

Deal, D. A. *The Nexus*. Georgia: ISAC Press, 1993.

Des Brisay, M. B. *History of the County of Lunenburg*. Bridgewater, Nova Scotia: The Bridgewater Bulletin Ltd., 1967.

Enterline, J. R. *Viking America*. London: NEL Mentor, 1974.

Evans, M. *Nova Scotia's Oak Island — The Unsolved Mystery*. Tantalon, Nova Scotia: Four East Publications, 1989.

Fanthorpe, R. L. and P. A. *The Holy Grail Revealed — The Real Secret of Rennes-le-Château*. San Bernardino, California: Borgo Press, 1986 edition.

Fanthorpe, R. L. and P. A. *Rennes-le-Château: Its Mysteries and Secrets*. Sunbury on Thames, Middlesex,UK: (Unit E4 Sunbury International Business Centre, Brooklands Close, TW16 7DX) Bellevue Books, 1991.(UK edition)

Fanthorpe, R. L. and P. A. *Secrets of Rennes-le-Château*. York Beach, Maine: Samuel Weiser Inc., 1992. (USA edition)

Finley, M. I. *Aspects of Antiquity — Discoveries and Controversies*. London: Pelican, 1977.

Foster, R. *The Complete Guide to Middle-Earth*. New York: Ballantine Books, 1978.

Furneaux, R. *Money Pit: The Mystery of Oak Island*. London: Fontana, 1976.

Guerber, H. A. *Myths of the Norsemen*. New York: Dover, 1992.

Guinness, A. E. *Mysteries of the Bible*. London: Hodder and Stoughton, 1988.

Hancock, G. *The Sign and the Seal*. London: Mandarin, 1993.

Harris, R.V. *The Oak Island Mystery*. Toronto: McGraw-Hill, Ryerson Ltd., 1958.

Hassrick, R.B. *North American Indians*. New Jersey: Octopus Books, 1975.

Higenbottam, F. *Codes and Ciphers*. English Universities Press, 1973.

Hitching, F. *The World Atlas of Mysteries*. London: Collins, 1978.

Holmer, P.L. *C. S. Lewis — The Shape of His Faith and Thought*. London: Sheldon Press, 1976.

Howard, T. *C. S. Lewis — Man of Letters*. Worthing, England: Churchman Publishing, 1987.

Hughes, J. (ed.). *The World Atlas of Archaeology*. London: Mitchell Beazley, 1988.

James, S. *Missing Pharaohs: Missing Tombs*. London: Maxbow, 1986.

James, S. *The Treasure Maps of Rennes-le-Château*. London: Maxbow, 1984.

Jenkins, L. *Elizabeth the Great*. London: Gollancz, 1958.

Johnson, L. *Revealed: The Secret of Oak Island*. Vancouver: Benwell Atkins, 1991.

Jones, Brinley R., (Ed.). *Anatomy of Wales*. Glamorgan, Wales: (Peterston-super-Ely), Gwerin Publications, 1972.

Kent, J.P.C. and Painter, K.S. *Wealth of the Roman World*. London: British Museum Publications Ltd., 1977.

Kilby, C. S. *C. S. Lewis — A Mind Awake*. New York: Harcourt Brace, 1980.

Knight, S. *The Brotherhood*. London: Granada, 1983.

Lacy, N. J. *The Arthurian Encyclopedia*. Woodbridge, Suffolk, U.K: Boydell Press, 1986.

Leary, T. P. *The Oak Island Enigma*. Omaha, Nebraska: Leary Publications, 1953.

Lewis, C. S. *Of This and Other Worlds*. London: Collins, 1982.

Lewis, C. S. *That Hideous Strength*. London: Pan Books, 1980 edition.

Lewis, C. S. *The Dark Tower*. London: Fount Paperbacks, 1983.

Lewis, C. S. *The World's Last Night and Other Essays*. New York: HBJ, 1960.

Lincoln, H. *The Holy Place*. London: Jonathan Cape Ltd., 1991.

Longfellow, H. W. *The Poetical Works*. London: Yardley and Hanscomb, c.1900.

McCarry, Charles and Gahan, G. "Nova Scotia, the Magnificent Anchorage." *National Geographic*, (Volume 147, Number 3): 334.

MacDonald, George. *Lilith*. London: Lion Publishing, 1982 reprint.

MacDonald, George. *Phantastes*. London: Lion Publishing, 1982 reprint.

MacLear, G. F. *Old Testament History*. London: Macmillan, 1899.

Mahan, Joseph B. *North American Sun Kings*. Georgia, U.S.A.: ISAC Press, 1992.

Mann, W. *Nova Scotia: The New Jerusalem*. Unpublished manuscript.

Marzials, F. (translator). *Memoirs of the Crusades*. London: J.M.Dent, Everyman Edition, 1908.

Mason, A.E.W. *The Life of Francis Drake*. London: Hodder and Stoughton, 1943.

Matheson, P.E. and E.F. *Francis Bacon — Selections*. London: Milford, 1922.

Mercer, D. *Exploring Unspoilt Britain*. London: Octopus Books for the National Trust, 1985.

Mitchell, D. *Pirates*. London: Thames and Hudson, 1976.

Morlet, A. *Origines de l'Ecriture*. Montpelier, France, (7 Rue Dom-Vaissette): Cause, Graille & Castelnau, 1955.

Nichols, P.B. and Moon, P. *The Montauk Project*. New York: Sky Books, 1992.

Noel, R.S. *The Mythology of Middle-Earth*. London: Thames and Hudson, 1977.

Norvill, Roy. *The Treasure Seeker's Treasury*. London: Hutchinson, 1978.

O'Connor, D. *The Money Pit: The Story of Oak Island and the World's Greatest Treasure Hunt*. New York: Coward, McCann and Geohagen, Inc., 1978.
O'Connor, D. *The Big Dig*. New York: Ballantine Books, 1988.

Pope, D. *Harry Morgan's Way — The Biography of Sir Henry Morgan 1635 - 1684*. London: Secker and Warburg, 1977.

Potts, H. *Francis Bacon and his Secret Society*. London: Sampson Low, Marston and Co., 1891.

Raeper, W. *George MacDonald, Novelist and Victorian Visionary*. London: Lion Publishing, 1988.

Robin, J. *Opération Orth, ou l'Incroyable Secret de Rennes-le-Château*. Paris: Editions de la Maisnie, 1989.

Saunière, E. *Moi, Bérenger Saunière*. Rennes-le-Château, France: Saunière Publications, 1989.

Shaw, M.R.B. (translator). *Chronicles of the Crusades*. London: Penguin, 1983.

Sinclair, A. *The Sword and the Grail*. London: Century, 1993.

Sitchin, Z. *The Lost Realms*. New York: Avon Books, 1990.

Sitchin, Z. *The Stairway to Heaven*. New York: Avon Books, 1980.

Sitchin, Z. *The 12th Planet*. New York: Avon Books, c.1978.

Sitchin, Z. *The Wars of Gods and Men*. New York: Avon Books, 1985.

Sitchin, Z. *When Time Began*. New York: Avon Books, 1993.

Smith, E. A. *Myths of the Iroquois*. Ohsweken, Ontario, Canada (RR Number 2, NOA IMO): Iroquois Publications, 1989.

Smith, W., and Fuller, J.M. *A Dictionary of the Bible, (Four Volumes)*. London: John Murray, 1893.

Snow, E.R. *Strange Tales from Nova Scotia to Cape Hatteras*. New York: Dodd, Mead and Co., 1949.

Spence, Lewis. *Myths and Legends of Ancient Egypt*. London: G. Harrap, 1915.

Steiger, S., Bielek, A. and Hanson Steiger, S. *The Philadelphia Experiment and Other UFO Conspiracies*. New Brunswick: Inner Light Publications, 1990.

Tucker, R. *Strange Gospels*. London: Harper Collins, 1989.

Tyler, J.E.A. *The Tolkien Companion*. London: Pan, 1976.

Wallis Budge, E.A. *An Egyptian Hieroglyph Dictionary* (Two Volumes), New York: Dover, 1978 reprint of 1920 original.

Wallis Budge, E.A. *Egyptian Language*. New York: Dover, 1983 reprint of 1910 original.

Wallis Budge, E.A. *The Book of the Dead*. Secaucus, New Jersey: The Citadel Press, 1984 reprint.

Warner, P. *The Medieval Castle*. London: Weidenfeld and Nicolson, 1971.

Wendt, H. *From Ape to Adam*. London: Thames and Hudson, 1972.

Wilkins, Harold T. *Captain Kidd and His Skeleton Island*. New York: Liveright Publishing Co., 1937.

Williams, N. *Francis Drake*. London: Weidenfeld and Nicolson, 1973.

Wilson, D. *The World Atlas of Treasure*. London: Pan, 1981.

Wilson, A.N. *C.S. Lewis — A Biography*, London: Flamingo (Harper Collins), 1990.

Winston, A. *No Purchase, No Pay*. London: Eyre and Spottiswoode, 1970.

Wise, Leonard F. *World Rulers*. London: Ward Lock, 1967.

Young, George. *Ancient Peoples and Modern Ghosts*. Queensland, Nova Scotia: George Young Publications, 1980.

Young, George. *Ghosts in Nova Scotia*. Queensland, Nova Scotia: George Young Publications, 1977.

Index